PREFACE

1. Scope

This publication provides doctrine for financial management in support of joint operations, to include multinational and interagency financial coordination considerations.

2. Purpose

This publication has been prepared under the direction of the Chairman of the Joint Chiefs of Staff. It sets forth joint doctrine to govern the activities and performance of the Armed Forces of the United States in joint operations and provides the doctrinal basis for interagency coordination and for US military involvement in multinational operations. It provides military guidance for the exercise of authority by combatant commanders and other joint force commanders (JFCs) and prescribes joint doctrine for operations, education, and training. It provides military guidance for use by the Armed Forces in preparing their appropriate plans. It is not the intent of this publication to restrict the authority of the JFC from organizing the force and executing the mission in a manner the JFC deems most appropriate to ensure unity of effort in the accomplishment of the overall objective.

3. Application

a. Joint doctrine established in this publication applies to the Joint Staff, commanders of combatant commands, subunified commands, joint task forces, subordinate components of these commands, and the Services.

b. The guidance in this publication is authoritative; as such, this doctrine will be followed except when, in the judgment of the commander, exceptional circumstances dictate otherwise. If conflicts arise between the contents of this publication and the contents of Service publications, this publication will take precedence unless the Chairman of the Joint Chiefs of Staff, normally in coordination with the other members of the Joint Chiefs of Staff, has provided more current and specific guidance. Commanders of forces operating as part of a multinational (alliance or coalition) military command should follow multinational doctrine and procedures ratified by the United States. For doctrine and procedures not ratified by the United States, commanders should evaluate and follow the multinational command's doctrine and procedures where applicable and consistent with US law, regulations, and doctrine.

For the Chairman of the Joint Chiefs of Staff:

WILLIAM E. GORTNEY
VADM, USN
Director, Joint Staff

- **Deletes references to United States Joint Force Command and the Business Transformation Agency as these organizations are being disestablished.**

- **Updates the "Defense Enterprise Management System" to the "Defense Enterprise Accounting and Management System."**

- **Removes references to "assessment tools" under currency control and support mechanisms as a subset of banking and disbursing support.**

- **Deletes Appendix H, "Financial Management Provisions for Theater Support Contracting Action."**

- **Deletes references to the Defense Integrated Military Human Resources System for Personnel and Pay.**

- **Removes the United Nations from the list of "Financial Operations Stakeholders" in the Reference Appendix.**

- **Removes description of nongovernmental organizations and the United States Institute for Peace from the "Interagency Coordination" section of the Reference Appendix.**

- **Deletes extensive description of Civil-Military Operations Center operations in the Reference Appendix.**

Intentionally Blank

TABLE OF CONTENTS

- **Provides an Overview of Financial Management Support**

- **Describes Roles, Responsibilities, and Organization**

- **Explains the Essential Elements of Resource Management**

- **Discusses the Essential Elements of Finance Support**

Overview of Financial Management Support

Commanders must understand the importance of financial management (FM) to successfully execute military operations.

Financial management (FM) complements combat power, supports strategic and operational reach, and enables endurance. Every mission requires a variety of funding sources and authorities. In addition, financial managers may provide decision support and funds control while executing the joint acquisition process with US and foreign currency.

Purpose of FM

FM supports accomplishment of the joint force commander's (JFC's) mission by providing two different, but mutually supporting, core functions: resource management (RM) and finance support. **RM** includes providing advice and recommendations to the commander; developing command resource requirements; identifying sources of funds; determining costs; acquiring funds; distributing and controlling funds; tracking costs and obligations; capturing costs; establishing reimbursement procedures; and establishing management internal controls. **Finance support** includes providing financial advice and recommendations; supporting the procurement process; providing limited pay support; and providing disbursing support.

FM Executive Agent

The executive agent (EA) for FM normally will fund multi-Service contract costs, unique joint force operational costs, special programs, joint force headquarters (HQ) operational costs, and any other designated support costs. During joint operation planning, the subordinate JFC must designate what the EA for FM will be required to fund and what the Service components must fund, based on supported combatant commander (CCDR) guidance.

Objectives of Joint FM	Four joint FM objectives support mission accomplishment:
	Provide commanders with the necessary information to make resource informed decisions and then obtain mission-essential funding quickly and efficiently.
	Reduce the impact of insufficient funding on readiness.
	Ensure fiscal year integrity and avoid anti-deficiency violations.
	Conduct detailed FM planning and coordinate efforts between the Services and combatant commands to provide and sustain resources.
Principles of Joint FM	The principles of joint FM are:
The application of principles of joint FM will contribute to development of an appropriate and successful FM concept of support.	Integrate FM responsibilities of Department of Defense (DOD) components and operational requirements of the CCDRs.
	Provide consistent FM guidance in support of joint operations.
	Ensure consistency of finance support to joint force personnel.
	Commanders prioritize and allocate resources seeking to optimize the effective and efficient use in accomplishing the assigned mission.

Roles, Responsibilities, and Organization

Office of the Secretary of Defense FM Responsibilities	The Under Secretary of Defense for Policy (USD[P]) has responsibility within DOD for certain contingency operations (peace operations, foreign humanitarian assistance [FHA], and noncombatant evacuation operations). The Under Secretary of Defense (Comptroller/Chief Financial Officer) (USD[C/CFO]) is responsible for overall financial policy for contingency operations and works with USD(P) to determine the most responsive method of financing. Defense Finance and Accounting Service (DFAS) has the responsibility for DOD finance and accounting policies, procedures, standards, systems, and operations in support of the combatant commands and Services. The Services are the proponents for FM and provide guidance and implementing instructions regarding all FM issues. United States Special

Operations Command (USSOCOM) provides management and authority on use of Major Force Program-11 funding. The Services and USSOCOM allocate funds appropriated for programs established by Congress, monitor their execution, and recommend major reprogramming of funds.

Chairman of the Joint Chiefs of Staff FM Responsibilities

The Chairman of the Joint Chiefs of Staff is responsible for transmitting the Secretary of Defense orders to CCDRs, including a funding paragraph outlining the financial responsibilities, as directed by the USD(C/CFO) and Under Secretary of Defense for Policy (USD[P]), and a logistics annex providing organizational identification of logistic responsibility.

Combatant Command Comptroller

The goal of having a combatant command comptroller is to provide a single point of contact with a staff element to oversee all FM requirements for the CCDR and to act as a liaison to subordinate commanders.

Subordinate Joint Force Command Comptroller

The joint force comptroller normally is part of the JFC's personal or special staff group. Although the component commanders have the primary responsibility for providing resources, the joint force comptroller is responsible for integrating joint force-wide RM and finance support policy planning and execution efforts.

Joint Force Component Commanders' FM Responsibilities

Joint force component commanders' FM responsibilities include: acquire, manage, distribute, and control funds and monitor execution, and take corrective action as necessary; and, prepare cost estimates and submit budget justifications to higher HQ organizations.

Resource Management

Resource managers must be involved early in resource management (RM) planning to ensure success.

RM is an ongoing analysis of the commander's tasks and priorities to identify and ensure that adequate and proper financial resources are available and applied under appropriate management controls to aid success.

Essential Elements of RM

Although each contingency operation has a unique set of RM parameters associated with its execution, all of the following essential elements of RM will be involved: providing financial advice and recommendations to the commander, developing command resource requirements, identifying sources of funding, determining costs, acquiring funds, distributing and controlling funds, tracking costs and obligations, capturing costs, conducting reimbursement procedures, accounting and fiscal validation, establishing management internal control, establishing a financial assistance visit and inspection process, and providing accurate and complete accounting support.

Develop Command Resource Requirements

It is important that the command resource requirements adequately reflect the concept of logistic support. Resource requirements include, but are not limited to, contracting, transportation, multinational support, support to interagency partners, intergovernmental organizations, FHA, and force sustainment.

Identify Sources of Funding

Funding a joint operation can present a challenge because of diverse fiscal requirements, sources, and authorities of funds. Multiple funding sources and authorities must be sought to balance constraints imposed by fiscal law with emergent time-critical operational requirements.

Determine Costs

the formula for determining a joint operation's cost is calculated as follows:

Total Costs – (Baseline Costs + Offset Costs) = Incremental Costs

Cost Capture Procedures

Resource managers will establish reporting procedures for their command's subordinate units to report their estimated or actual commitments, obligations, reimbursable costs, and estimated future costs. The ability to report to Congress on the use of appropriated and nonappropriated funds is critical in meeting the EA's responsibility for stewardship of public resources. Effective cost capturing is achieved through a joint effort between finance and RM personnel.

Provide Accurate and Complete Accounting Support

The joint force comptroller supports the Service comptroller in ensuring official accounting records are accurate, properly supported by source documentation, and resolving accounting issues in a timely manner.

Finance Support

Effective finance support provides the financial resources necessary for successful mission accomplishment.

Finance support during joint operations ensures banking and currency support for personnel payments, theater support contracting, and other special programs. It involves financial analysis and recommendations to help the JFC make the most efficient use of fiscal resources.

Essential Elements of Finance Support	Though each contingency operation has a unique set of parameters associated with its execution, all operations involve the essential elements of finance support that provide financial advice and recommendations; support the procurement process; provide pay support; and, provide banking and disbursing support.
Provide Financial Advice and Recommendations	The joint force comptroller must obtain and analyze the economic assessment of the operational environment and begin initial coordination with the DFAS Crisis Coordination Center. The DFAS Crisis Coordination Center will provide advice and act as the primary DFAS liaison. The joint force comptroller will recommend joint force FM policies and develop the concept of finance support outlined in the FM appendix to the joint operation plan or operation order.
Support the Procurement Process	Component finance units, when required, will provide funds for the local purchase of goods and services. Procurement support is divided into two areas: contracting support and commercial vendor services support.
Provide Pay Support	Pay support includes answering pay inquiries, initiating various types of individual local payments (e.g., casual payments, travel payments), check cashing, and local currency exchange.
Provide Banking and Disbursing Support	Disbursing support includes, but is not necessarily limited to, making various types of payments certified as correct and proper, check cashing, and local currency conversion.

CONCLUSION

This publication provides doctrine for FM in support of joint operations, to include multinational and interagency financial coordination considerations.

Intentionally Blank

CHAPTER I
OVERVIEW

> *"Operational risks are those associated with the current force executing the strategy successfully within acceptable human, material, financial, and strategic costs."*
>
> **National Defense Strategy, June 2008**

1. Introduction

a. The Armed Forces of the United States tailor operations to meet mission requirements. This is true not only when the military instrument of national power is the predominant option employed, but also when the other instruments of national power are the preferred option. Joint forces must be prepared to conduct operations across the range of military operations with a variety of Department of Defense (DOD) (e.g., Defense Logistics Agency) and other United States Government (USG) department and agencies (e.g., Federal Bureau of Investigation), allied and coalition forces, intergovernmental organizations (IGOs) (e.g., United Nations [UN]), and nongovernmental organizations (NGOs) (e.g., American Red Cross).

b. Commanders must understand the importance of financial management (FM) to successfully execute military operations. FM complements combat power, supports strategic and operational reach, and enables endurance. Every mission requires a variety of funding sources and authorities. In addition, financial managers may provide decision support and funds control while executing the joint acquisition process with US and foreign currency.

c. As a nation, the US wages war employing all instruments of national power—diplomatic, informational, military, and economic. Economic power can be an effective means for a nation and/or multinational force to combat incipient threats or entrenched, intransigent nations. At the strategic level, it is part of a whole-of-government approach to applying the instruments of national power as applicable.

d. Emerging from experiences gained during Operation ENDURING FREEDOM and Operation IRAQI FREEDOM are processes and procedures being employed by joint force commanders (JFCs) and their staffs in planning, executing, and assessing efforts to integrate financial operations into their joint operation/campaign plans. Integrated financial operations (IFOs) have two major aspects: funding of economic development and infrastructure projects to win the support of a local population and to separate that population from an insurgency; and contributing to destroying the insurgents' financial networks. IFO seeks to refine processes and procedures that improve the integration and prioritization efforts among the USG departments and agencies, multinational forces, IGOs, and NGOs.

e. DOD works with other USG departments and agencies and with partner nations to deny, disrupt, or defeat and degrade adversaries' ability to use illicit financial networks to negatively affect US interests. Combatant commanders (CCDRs), when authorized and where appropriate, should support interagency threat finance efforts to diminish the capabilities of adversary groups and criminal networks through the denial of funding and value transfer items. They should also, in collaboration with interagency partners, establish mechanisms with other nations to deny, disrupt, destroy, or defeat funding and value transfer items to adversaries. JFCs and their staffs should gain and maintain situational awareness of these ongoing efforts as they formulate their own IFO to leverage ongoing efforts and ensure their own plans support other USG operations.

2. Purpose of Financial Management

a. FM supports accomplishment of the JFC's mission by providing two different, but mutually supporting, core functions: resource management (RM) and finance support (see Figure I-1). RM includes providing advice and recommendations to the commander; developing command resource requirements; identifying sources of funds; determining costs; acquiring funds; distributing and controlling funds; tracking costs and obligations; capturing costs; establishing reimbursement procedures; and establishing management internal controls. Finance support includes providing financial advice and recommendations; supporting the procurement process; providing limited pay support; and providing disbursing support.

b. RM and finance support will be discussed further in Chapter III, "Resource Management," and Chapter IV, "Finance Support," respectively.

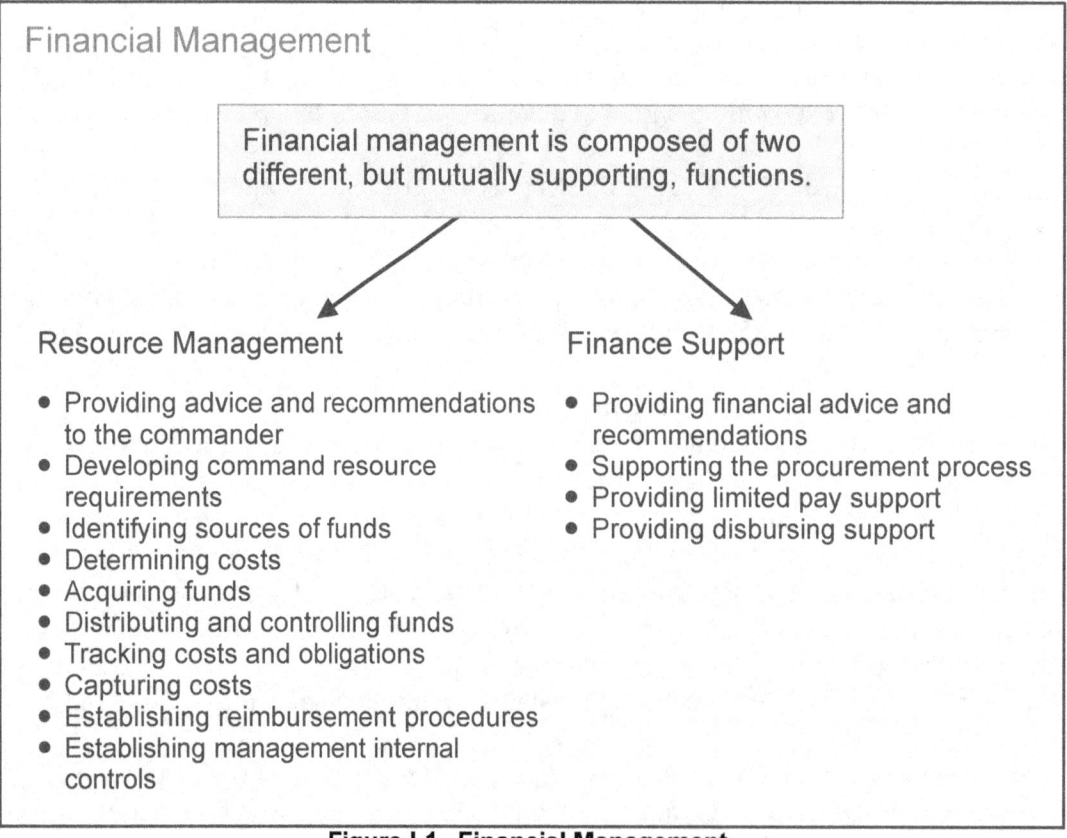

Figure I-1. Financial Management

3. Financial Management Executive Agent

a. The Secretary of Defense (SecDef) may elect to designate an executive agent (EA) in accordance with Department of Defense Directive (DODD) 5101.1, *DOD Executive Agent.* This EA normally is the Secretary of a Military Department. The supported CCDR identifies the designated EA for FM in the joint operation plan (OPLAN) or operation order (OPORD).

b. The EA for FM normally will fund multi-Service contract costs, unique joint force operational costs, special programs, joint force headquarters (HQ) operational costs, and any other designated support costs. DOD components will fund their predeployment, deployment, operating tempo (OPTEMPO), sustainment, redeployment, reconstitution, and military personnel costs. During joint operation planning the subordinate JFC, based on supported CCDR guidance, must designate what the EA for FM will be required to fund and what the Service components must fund. When required by DOD, separate cost accounts are established to capture direct costs incurred in support of other organizations such as coalition forces and NGOs.

4. Stewardship

DOD is entrusted by the American people as steward of the vital resources (personnel, funds, materiel, land, facilities) provided to defend the nation. All available resources shall be used in the most efficient means possible.

5. Objectives of Joint Financial Management

Purpose. The establishment of joint FM objectives facilitates unified action and the prudent use of resources. Four joint FM objectives that support mission accomplishment are discussed hereafter:

a. Provide commanders with the necessary information to make resource informed decisions and then obtain mission-essential funding as quickly and efficiently as possible using the proper source and authority of funds as directed in applicable guidance and agreements.

b. Reduce the impact of insufficient funding on readiness. Financial managers can accomplish this through such actions as seeking alternative funding sources, recommending no cost alternatives, and ensuring that accurate cost estimates are provided to assist in the timely reimbursement of Service component appropriated expenses.

c. Ensure fiscal year integrity and avoid anti-deficiency violations. Fiscal year integrity and possible anti-deficiency violations are a legal concern in joint operations. These concerns are more pronounced when substantial contingencies occur in the third or fourth quarter. Basic fiscal controls on appropriated funds are essential to protect against Antideficiency Act violations. The following basic fiscal controls should be adhered to:

(1) Obligations and expenditures are incurred only by authorized individuals and only with proper authorization (e.g., execute order).

(2) Obligations are incurred only after an appropriation or continuing resolution has been passed by Congress.

(3) Obligations are incurred within the purpose, time, and amount limits applicable to the appropriation.

d. Conduct detailed FM planning and coordinate efforts between the Services and combatant commands to provide and sustain resources. In addition, unity of effort in a joint environment demands an increased financial situational awareness and will often include collaborative work across the joint, interagency, intergovernmental, and multinational arenas. See Appendix K, "Integrated Financial Operations Planning Considerations."

6. Principles of Joint Financial Management

a. **General.** To effectively support the joint operation, FM must be proactive and responsive in identifying and securing funding to meet operational requirements. The principles discussed below are based on sound concepts and operational experience. Their application will contribute to development of an appropriate and successful FM concept of support.

b. **Financial Management Principles**

(1) Integrate FM responsibilities of DOD components and operational requirements of the CCDRs. As depicted in Figure I-2, the supported CCDR may choose to conduct joint operations through subordinate JFCs, Service component commanders, or functional component commanders. However, funding for joint operations flows through either a Military Department, United States Special Operations Command (USSOCOM), or a DOD agency. Joint financial managers must understand the mechanics of this reality and be able to integrate those unique FM responsibilities associated with joint operations.

(2) Provide consistent FM guidance in support of joint operations. This includes being involved in the staff estimate process, developing appendix 3 (Finance and Disbursing) to annex E (Personnel) in a joint OPLAN or OPORD and, when necessary, conducting an economic analysis of the joint operations area (JOA).

See Appendix C, "Guide to Operation Plan Development."

(3) Ensure consistency of finance support to joint force personnel. DOD and the Services financial managers will coordinate to ensure consistent finance support is provided to all joint force members. This includes making appropriate provisions for limited military pay and services, establishing banking and currency support, payment of travel entitlements, and cash operations to support the acquisition process.

(4) Commanders prioritize and allocate resources seeking to optimize the effective and efficient use in accomplishing the assigned mission.

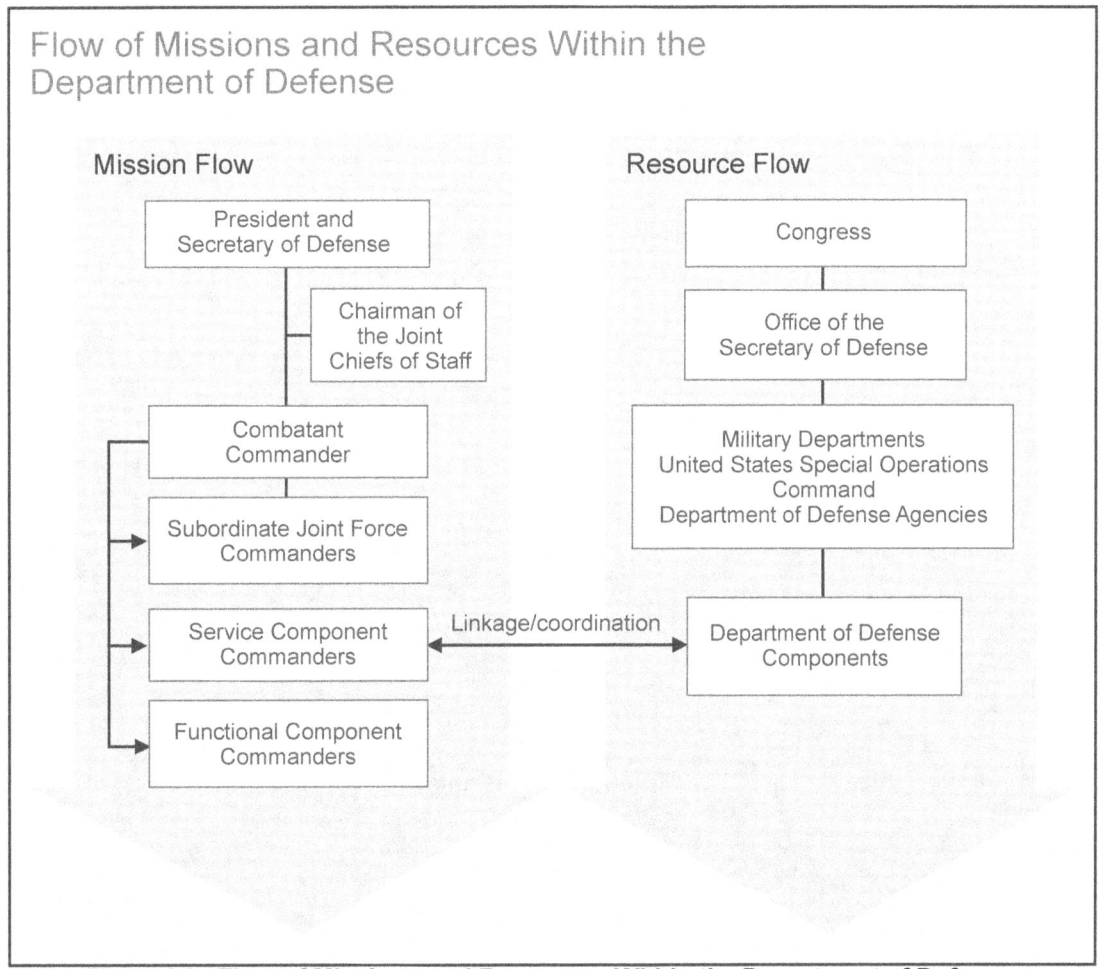

Figure I-2. Flow of Missions and Resources Within the Department of Defense

Intentionally Blank

CHAPTER II
ROLES, RESPONSIBILITIES, AND ORGANIZATION

> *"The joint force comptroller management of these elements [resource management and finance support] provides the JFC [joint force commander] with many necessary capabilities: from contracting and banking support to cost capturing and fund control."*
>
> **Joint Publication 3-0, Joint Operations**

1. Office of the Secretary of Defense Financial Management Responsibilities

a. Joint operations involve a vast web of comptroller and RM agencies. This includes those FM personnel attached to elements of the joint force and those supporting the joint force operation through reachback capabilities, regardless of location.

b. Appendix A, "Financial Management Responsibilities within the Department of Defense," identifies other key DOD participants and their responsibilities for successful FM planning and execution.

2. Chairman of the Joint Chiefs of Staff Financial Management Responsibilities

a. The Chairman of the Joint Chiefs of Staff (CJCS) is responsible for transmitting SecDef orders to CCDRs, including a funding paragraph outlining the financial responsibilities, as directed by the Under Secretary of Defense (Comptroller/Chief Financial Officer)(USD[C/CFO]) and Under Secretary of Defense for Policy (USD[P]), and a logistics annex providing organizational identification of logistic responsibility.

b. CJCS provides an execute order to a supported CCDR describing mission requirements. Normally, the supported and supporting CCDRs' Service components will fund their participation in an operation with operation and maintenance (O&M) funds. However, other appropriations may be used to support a given operation.

c. CJCS also is responsible for managing the Combatant Commander Initiative Fund (CCIF), acting as approval authority as provided in Title 10, United States Code (USC), Section 166a, formulating policies for program administration, and providing reports to Congress as requested.

3. Combatant Command Comptroller

a. **Roles.** CCDRs organize their staffs and assign responsibilities as necessary to facilitate unified action and accomplishment of assigned missions. Accordingly, the combatant command comptroller may be a principal staff officer (i.e., directorate), a subordinate staff officer in the logistics directorate of a joint staff (J-4) or another directorate of a joint staff, or the leader of a personal or special staff section under the chief of staff or deputy commander. The goal, however, is the same—to provide a single point of contact with a staff element to oversee all FM requirements for the CCDR and to act as a liaison to subordinate commanders.

b. **Responsibilities**

(1) Serve as the CCDR's principal advisor on FM matters.

(2) Coordinate with the Joint Staff, supporting CCDRs' comptrollers, and supporting USG departments and agencies to ensure timely receipt of FM instructions and authorities.

(3) Provide funding guidance and, when necessary, coordinate with the Joint Staff and SecDef for designation of an EA.

(4) Prepare staff estimates and appendix 3 (Finance and Disbursing) to annex E (Personnel) in OPLANs and OPORDs.

(5) Transfer responsibilities to the joint force comptroller as soon as possible after activation of the joint task force (JTF). This includes updating the joint force comptroller on the status of funding actions, financial support, and other mission-unique requirements.

(6) Coordinate with the supported and supporting USG departments and agencies and promulgate appropriate reimbursement procedures.

(7) Coordinate with the operations directorate of a joint staff at the combatant command level and Service component commands to ensure early deployment of finance units into the operational area.

(8) Identify required funding authorities.

(9) Provide execution data and funding projections for any operations occurring in the area of responsibility (AOR).

4. **Subordinate Joint Force Command Comptroller**

a. **Roles**

(1) The joint force comptroller normally is part of the JFC's personal or special staff group. The joint force comptroller, along with the supported CCDR's comptroller, must be involved early in joint operation planning to clearly define FM responsibilities. Although the component commanders have the primary responsibility for providing resources, the joint force comptroller is responsible for integrating joint force-wide RM and finance support policy planning and execution efforts. The JFC may designate a component commander's comptroller or finance staff officer to also serve as the joint force comptroller.

(2) A key role for the comptroller is to ensure a process is established (in general, a joint acquisition review board [JARB] or joint facilities utilization board [JFUB]) to facilitate

the boarding of identified requirements. This ensures requirements are within required contracting/approval and threshold parameters. The comptroller then sources the funding to execute them. Inherent in this is the comptroller's close coordination with the logistics, legal, and contracting staff sections to integrate requirements with contracting/funding.

(a) The JARB coordinates and controls the requirements generation and prioritization of joint common-user logistics (CUL) supplies and services needed for the operational mission. It is normally chaired by the JFC, deputy commander, or J-4. The JARB's main role is to make specific approval and prioritization recommendations for all geographic combatant commander (GCC)-directed, subordinate JFC-controlled, high-value and/or high-visibility CUL requirements and to include recommendations on the proper source of support for these requirements.

(b) The JFUB evaluates and reconciles component requests for real estate, use of existing facilities, inter-Service support, and construction to ensure compliance with joint civil-military engineering board priorities (if established).

b. **Responsibilities**

(1) Serve as the JFC's principal FM advisor and focal point for JTF FM matters.

(2) Prepare appendix 3 (Finance and Disbursing) to annex E (Personnel) for OPLANs and OPORDs.

See Appendix C, "Guide to Operation Plan Development."

(3) Establish joint force FM responsibilities. Based on the missions and geographic locations of the joint force components, the joint force comptroller may coordinate the designation of a lead agent(s) for specific FM functions, special support requirements, or a specific location.

(4) Review estimated and actual costs of the joint operation when available and provide recommendations for addressing differences.

(5) Establish management internal controls to ensure the efficient and appropriate use of resources.

(6) Coordinate the joint force entitlement policy (pay and allowances), through the joint force manpower and personnel directorate of a joint staff (J-1), with the GCC's J-1. This includes the GCC determination of the appropriate temporary duty (TDY) option for joint force personnel.

(7) Coordinate with joint force J-4 on logistic and contracting requirements to ensure they complement FM responsibilities. Participate in the joint force J-4 planning groups and boards, as required.

(8) Coordinate with other joint force staff members concerning their FM requirements and provide them guidance on meeting their FM responsibilities.

(9) Determine sources of funds and obligation authority. Review any applicable agreements that require FM support.

(10) Coordinate with contracting officials to verify funding availability for local contracting needs and determine contract payment requirements.

(11) Coordinate with the Service components supporting the JFC to ensure early deployment of finance personnel into the JOA. The purpose is to support the immediate contracting requirements of the deploying force that are not readily available from other USG sources.

(12) Coordinate, when necessary, the designation of a limited depository account (LDA) in accordance with DOD 7000.14-R, Department of Defense Financial Management Regulations (DODFMRs), Volume 5, *Disbursing Policy and Procedures*. DOD 7000.14-R is commonly known as DODFMR, which is used throughout the remainder of this publication.

c. **Organization and Functions**

(1) **Organization.** The actual composition will be dictated by the overall joint force organization and types of operations.

(2) **Functions.** The following are specific functions of the joint force comptroller organization:

(a) **RM Policy Section**

<u>1</u>. Participates in the staff estimate process and develops appendix 3 (Finance and Disbursing) to annex E (Personnel) in the joint OPLAN or OPORD.

See Appendix C, "Guide to Operation Plan Development."

<u>2</u>. Obtains and interprets economic analysis information.

<u>3</u>. Establishes FM procedures and ensures oversight and periodic review to ensure no violations of Title 31, USC, Sections 1517 or 1301 are committed.

<u>4</u>. Provides liaison with the Defense Finance and Accounting Service (DFAS) and Service components regarding account matters.

<u>5</u>. Conducts FM assistance visits and inspections.

6. Establishes, maintains, and reports annually on management internal controls.

(b) **RM Budget Section**

1. Identifies sources of funding.

See Appendix E, "Financial Appropriations and Authorities."

2. As required, utilizes funding authority, determines actual costs and estimates future costs, acquires funds, distributes and controls funds, tracks costs and obligations, and captures cost.

(c) **Finance Policy Section**

1. Coordinates pay entitlement policy with the joint force J-1.

2. Coordinates and establishes the joint force fund security and disbursing policies and guidance.

3. Coordinates local procurement support with the joint force J-4, joint contracting cell, and other staff principals having resource allocation responsibilities.

4. Obtains and interprets economic analysis information.

(d) **Finance Funding Section**

1. Coordinates host nation (HN) banking support.

2. Supports the procurement process with needed currency.

(e) Liaison officers from the components and representatives from DFAS may augment and assist the staff of the joint force comptroller.

5. Joint Force Component Commanders' Financial Management Responsibilities

a. Acquire, manage, distribute, and control funds and monitor execution, and take corrective action as necessary.

b. Prepare cost estimates and submit budget justifications to higher HQ organizations.

c. Track costs and obligations and provide monthly incremental reports through appropriate channels to DFAS, as required, and to the USD(C/CFO) and the Director for Force Structure, Resource, and Assessment, Joint Staff (J-8).

d. Provide billing documents to DFAS in those instances where reimbursement is requested.

CHAPTER III
RESOURCE MANAGEMENT

"To carry out war three things are necessary: money, money, and yet more money."

Marshal Gian Giacomo Trivulzio
to Louis XII of France in 1499

1. Overview

a. Generally, RM is an ongoing analysis of the commander's tasks and priorities to identify and ensure that adequate and proper financial resources are available and applied under appropriate management controls to aid success. Resource managers must be involved early in RM planning to ensure success. Because joint operations vary greatly in scope and duration, RM must be flexible to support changing requirements. The joint force comptroller and component resource managers may be required to identify, allocate, distribute, control, and report fund execution for certain funding authorities. However, RM primarily will occur at the Service component command level. As the senior resource manager, the joint force comptroller also advises the commander on the best allocation of resources during the staff estimate process. Depending on a specific mission's complexity and anticipated duration, joint force comptroller RM duties may include directing or coordinating the financial analysis of planned operations; ensuring the effective and efficient use of funding resources during execution; and developing and maintaining close coordination with the joint force J-4, contracting personnel, legal advisor, and DFAS. The joint force comptroller will also be involved in various assessment activities to evaluate the effectiveness of RM, recommend changes, and compile lessons learned for future use. Actionable lessons learned and best practices should be forwarded to the appropriate joint community of practice in the Joint Lessons Learned Information System for dissemination and subsequent analysis.

b. RM functions will be performed during all military operations. A joint force comptroller checklist, furnished in Appendix B, "Joint Force Comptroller Checklist," provides, by phase of a military operation, recommended RM planning and execution considerations.

2. Essential Elements of Resource Management

a. **General.** Although each contingency operation has a unique set of RM parameters associated with its execution, all of the following essential elements of RM will be involved: providing financial advice and recommendations to the commander, developing command resource requirements, identifying sources of funding, determining costs, acquiring funds, distributing and controlling funds, tracking costs and obligations, capturing costs, conducting reimbursement procedures, accounting and fiscal validation, establishing management internal control, establishing a financial assistance visit and inspection process, and providing accurate and complete accounting support.

b. **Provide RM advice and recommendations to the commander.** When authorized by SecDef, the supported CCDR will issue appropriate fiscal and logistical guidance to subordinate commanders. Accordingly, the joint force comptroller advises the JFC concerning the effective use of available resources and the EA's responsibilities. Financial managers then should participate early and actively in joint operation planning and specifically, joint planning groups, to assist in the successful integration of all FM efforts.

c. **Develop Command Resource Requirements**

(1) Budget estimates, operating budgets, and financial plans normally do not include costs incurred in support of unplanned contingency operations. Funding will be drawn from current appropriations and authority, unless provided by a reimbursable agreement with another government or IGO. Thus, it is necessary for each commander to absorb these costs initially from within existing funds. The Service component command resource managers have the responsibility for ensuring the capability exists for funding all participation costs, separating and collecting the incremental and total costs, and reporting these costs to DFAS and the Office of the Under Secretary of Defense (Comptroller/Chief Financial Officer) (OUSD[C/CFO]). To assist in reprogramming and supplemental funds requests, Service component command resource managers must estimate future costs, accumulate all costs, and promptly submit bills to DFAS for payment and estimated future costs to OUSD(C/CFO).

(2) When developing command resource requirements, existing agreements must be reviewed by the appropriate staff section. Based on this review, the Service component resource managers will ensure adherence to proper billing and reimbursement procedures. It is important that the command resource requirements adequately reflect the concept of logistic support. Resource requirements include, but are not limited to, contracting, transportation, multinational support, support to interagency partners, IGOs, foreign humanitarian assistance (FHA), and force sustainment.

(3) Host-nation support (HNS) can be a significant force multiplier. Whenever possible, available HNS should be considered as an alternative to deploying logistic support from the United States. HNS agreements should authorize the JFC to coordinate directly with the HN for support and acquisition, and for the use of facilities and real estate. The legal advisor must be involved in determining specific support requirements contained in HNS agreements. Authority for negotiations must be obtained through the supported CCDR, Joint Staff, DOD, and Department of State (DOS).

(4) Once a course of action (COA) is selected and preparation of the OPLAN or OPORD begins, the joint force comptroller develops RM policy and guidance to appendix 3 (Finance and Disbursing) to annex E (Personnel) of the OPLAN or OPORD. This appendix must also include which component is funding any unique aspects of the operation. The FM appendix should adequately reflect support of logistic requirements.

Refer to Appendix C, "Guide to Operation Plan Development," for guidance in the preparation of appendix 3 (Finance and Disbursing) to annex E (Personnel) of an OPLAN or OPORD.

d. **Identify Sources of Funding**

(1) Funding a joint operation can present a challenge because of diverse fiscal requirements, sources, and authorities of funds. Multiple funding sources and authorities must be sought to balance constraints imposed by fiscal law with emergent time-critical operational requirements. The joint force comptroller should work closely with the legal advisor when making these determinations to ensure compliance with Title 31, USC, Section 1301, which addresses use of funds for the purposes for which they are appropriated. Guidance from USD(C/CFO) spelled out in the DODFMR, Volume 12, *Special Accounts, Funds, and Programs,* Chapter 23, "Contingency Operations," should also be followed.

(2) Resource managers must also be aware of extraordinary measures, including emergency funding authorities such as the Feed and Forage Act (Title 41, USC, Section 11), which may be used to incur obligations in excess of, or in advance of, available appropriations. A thorough understanding of sources and authorities can provide resource managers with a means of remaining within the limits of the law and a method to develop alternative funding options. To the extent that a specific funding source has not been identified for a joint operation, Service component commanders should pursue additional funding authority, reprogramming, and supplemental appropriation requests to minimize the effect on component readiness.

See Appendix D, "Legal Considerations for Financial Management," for further information. Further, Appendix E, "Financial Appropriations and Authorities," contains a complete discussion of potential authorities and agreements.

e. **Determine Costs**

(1) For anticipated joint operations, preliminary cost estimates are developed before or early in the deployment of military forces by the OUSD(C/CFO), working in consonance with the Joint Staff, Services, USSOCOM, and DOD agencies and activities, as appropriate. DOD requests for supplemental funds or reprogramming are based on detailed budget estimates developed by the Services, USSOCOM, other combatant commands, and engaged DOD agencies and activities. As needed, resource managers should apply the policies contained in DODFMR, Volume 2, *Budget Formulation and Presentation,* that cover the estimated costs of additional personnel plus mutual logistic support with other countries and North Atlantic Treaty Organization (NATO) components.

(2) Preparing these estimates involves making assumptions about a variety of factors such as the joint operation's duration, logistic support, force size, operational environment, transportation, and special pay and allowances. Generally, all factors of mission, enemy, terrain and weather, troops and support available, time available, and civil considerations must be considered in developing assumptions and cost estimates. Costs are

estimated using standard cost factors developed from historical costs and judgment where there are no standard cost factors. This process requires input from various staff sections.

(3) Figure III-1 depicts the formula for determining a joint operation's cost. Services will utilize the "contingency cost report" format issued by USD(C/CFO) to provide DFAS and DOD with the joint operation's total incremental cost. Instructions for completing the contingency cost report can be found in DODFMR, Volume 12, *Special Accounts, Funds, and Programs,* Chapter 23, "Contingency Operations."

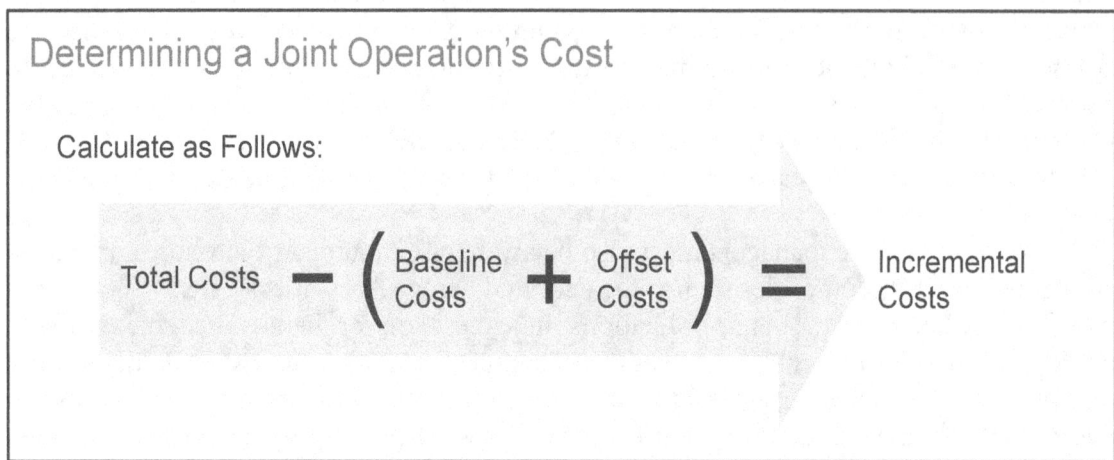

Figure III-1. Determining a Joint Operation's Cost

(4) When developing an estimate, misuse of terminology (e.g., confusing incremental and offset costs) can lead to an inaccurate cost estimate. An understanding and consistent use of these terms are essential when determining costs. The following are approved definitions of the terms in question:

(a) **Baseline Costs.** Baseline costs are the continuing annual costs of military operations funded by O&M and military personnel appropriations. Essentially, baseline costs are programmed and budgeted costs that would be incurred whether or not a contingency operation took place (e.g., scheduled flying hours, steaming days, training days, exercises).

(b) **Offset Costs.** In some instances, costs for which funds have been appropriated may not be incurred as a result of a contingency operation, and those funds may then be applied to the cost of the operation. Examples include basic allowance for subsistence not paid, training not conducted, and base operations support not provided. Reported incremental costs should be reduced by the amount of these cost offsets. In other situations, identified incremental costs may be offset in various ways, such as credit for unused classes of supply, and nonmonetary contributions, such as HN or multinational provided fuel. DODFMR Volume 12, *Special Accounts, Funds, and Programs,* Chapter 3, "Contributions for Defense Programs, Projects, and Activities," outlines procedures for reporting nonmonetary contributions. These offsets shall be accurately documented and reported at the cognizant organization levels to maintain adequate accountability for reporting and audit purposes.

(c) **Incremental Costs.** Incremental costs are additional costs to the appropriations and are only incurred upon execution of a contingency operation (see Figure III-2). DOD reports to Congress the incremental costs of its participation in contingency operations. Incremental costs do not include the cost of property or services acquired by DOD that was paid for by a source outside of DOD or out of funds contributed by such a source. The costs of investment items, construction costs, and costs incurred to fix existing shortcomings can be categorized as incremental expenses only if the expenditures were necessary to support a contingency operation and would not have been incurred in that fiscal year in the absence of the contingency requirement. The following are examples of incremental costs:

1. Military entitlements such as imminent danger pay, family separation allowance, or other payments made over and above the normal monthly payroll costs.

2. Increases in the amount of allowances due to changes in the geographic assignment area due to the joint operation (e.g., overseas housing allowance).

3. Travel and per diem costs of active duty military personnel.

4. Mobilization costs of members of the Reserve Component called to active duty and assigned solely to support the joint operation.

5. Overtime, travel, and per diem of permanent DOD civilian personnel in support of the joint operation.

Incremental Costs

Incremental costs are additional costs to the appropriations and are only incurred upon execution of a contingency operation.

- Military entitlements
- Allowance amount increases
- Travel and per diem costs
- Mobilization costs of Reserve components
- Overtime, travel, and per diem of permanent Department of Defense civilian personnel
- Wages, travel, and per diem of temporary Department of Defense civilian personnel
- Transportation costs
- Cost of rents, communications, and utilities
- Cost of work, services, training, and materiel
- Cost of materiel, equipment, and supplies
- Costs incurred which are paid from reimbursable funds
- Replacement costs of attrition losses
- Equipment overhaul and maintenance costs
- Component-specific costs for increased operational tempo

Figure III-2. Incremental Costs

      <u>6.</u> Wages, travel, and per diem of temporary DOD civilian personnel hired or assigned solely to perform services supporting the joint operation.

      <u>7.</u> Transportation costs of moving personnel, materiel, equipment, and supplies to the operation or staging area, including port handling charges; packing, crating, and handling; first and second destination charges; and other related areas. The exception is when the Commander, US Transportation Command, receives an order requiring transportation of non-US owned equipment and/or non-US personnel. In these instances, the Army will pay Military Surface Deployment and Distribution Command costs, the Navy will pay Military Sealift Command (MSC) costs, and the Air Force will pay Air Mobility Command costs.

      <u>8.</u> Cost of rents, communications, and utilities attributable to the joint operation (e.g., telephone service, computer and satellite time).

      <u>9.</u> Cost of work, services, training, and materiel procured under contract for the specific purpose of providing assistance in the joint operation.

      <u>10.</u> Cost of materiel, equipment, and supplies from regular stocks used in providing directed assistance. Materiel, equipment, and supplies from stock will be priced at the standard prices used for issue to DOD activities. Included in this category will be consumables such as field rations, medical supplies, office supplies, chemicals, petroleum, and items ordinarily consumed or expended within one year after they are put into use. Materiel, equipment, and supplies determined to be DOD excess may be made available for transfer under excess property disposal authority without reimbursement. However, in these instances, charges for packing, crating, and handling, and transportation will be added to the incremental cost.

      <u>11.</u> Costs incurred which are paid from the working capital of trust, revolving, or other funds whose reimbursement is required.

      <u>12.</u> Replacement costs of attrition losses directly attributable to support of the joint operation.

      <u>13.</u> The portion of equipment overhaul and maintenance costs that, when computed on a fractional use basis, reflect an additive cost attributable to the joint operation.

      <u>14.</u> Component-specific costs for increased OPTEMPO, such as steaming costs for the US Navy.

For more information on financial policy and procedures for contingency operations, see DODFMR, Volume 12, Special Accounts, Funds, and Programs, Chapter 23, "Contingency Operations."

    f. **Acquired Funds.** Once potential sources and authority of funds are determined, the Service component resource managers will request use of various funding authorities. In many cases, contingency operations require supplies and services not available to the JFC through the normal funding process. One example is funding for transportation required in support of FHA operations. Another example is funding available for special and specific missions such as urgent humanitarian relief and reconstruction requirements. In these cases, component resource managers will seek separate obligation authority through the appropriate channel.

g. **Distribute and Control Funds.** Normally, the distribution and control of funds remains with the Services. Procedures will adhere to US laws, regulations, and applicable policies. Effective and efficient fund control and certification is critical in the conduct of FM operations.

h. **Track Costs and Obligations.** Upon notification of an impending joint operation, each participating DOD component will develop special program codes for cost capture and reporting purposes. These relate to the three digit CJCS project code published for contingency operations.

i. **Cost Capture Procedures**

(1) Resource managers will establish reporting procedures for their command's subordinate units to report their estimated or actual commitments, obligations, reimbursable costs, and estimated future costs. Reporting procedures should be simple and flexible enough to ensure accurate reporting under any circumstances; nevertheless, each resource manager must comply with DOD reporting requirements. The component commander must be able to account for and receive reimbursement for the costs of supporting contingency operations by meeting three conditions. First, follow consistent and approved procedures in determining and calculating baseline and incremental costs recorded in accounting records. Second, use applicable special interest or program accounting codes, object class codes, and customer codes to trace costs. Third, use automated accounting systems that interface with a designated DFAS central billing system or provide a means to generate a manual bill. Resource managers will capture costs using existing finance and accounting systems and procedures. Cost reporting procedures are published by USD(C/CFO).

(2) Contingency cost reports are important for monitoring the adequacy of funding for such operations as well as for a variety of other purposes. They assist DOD in monitoring the resources necessary to support contingency operations and help determine the impact on readiness when drawing from previously appropriated funds to cover contingency costs. The reports help DOD develop supplemental appropriations requests, initiate funds reprogramming, and respond to congressional and public interest inquiries about contingency operations costs. In addition, the cost reports facilitate congressional oversight of the expenditure of appropriated funds and their assessment of the financial impact of contingency operations on DOD spending plans.

(3) The ability to report to Congress on the use of appropriated and nonappropriated funds is critical in meeting the EA's responsibility for stewardship of public resources. Appropriated and nonappropriated accounting requirements for a military

operation are immense, and they begin before the first deployment. The quality of accounting records depends primarily upon the timely receipt and accuracy of financial data. The level of accounting support depends upon the scale and complexity of the operation. Effective cost capturing is achieved through a joint effort between finance and RM personnel.

j. **Reimbursement Procedures**

(1) Reimbursable costs may occur from providing DOD support to IGOs, HNs, foreign nations, NGOs, or other USG departments and agencies. Provisions of said support must be authorized by law. Throughout operations, careful consideration must be given to funding, monitoring expenditure authority (see DODFMR, Volume 15, *Security Assistance Policy and Procedures,* Chapter 4, "Cash Management"), maintaining accountability, tracking costs, and tracking support received from, or provided to, the HN, IGOs, other foreign nations, or other USG departments and agencies. This is necessary to determine the detailed costs of an operation and to support the process of billing for reimbursement at all levels. Congress requires detailed reports on the projected and actual costs of contingency operations. Accurate, detailed cost reports are needed to determine how costs should be apportioned and billed. Financial managers will capture these costs and provide the required reports and detailed billings per DODFMR, Volume 11A and 11B, *Reimbursable Operations, Policy, and Procedures* (see Figure III-3).

(2) When support agreements are established by the CCDR or subordinate JFC, the joint force comptroller should ensure that it is clearly understood what assistance can be

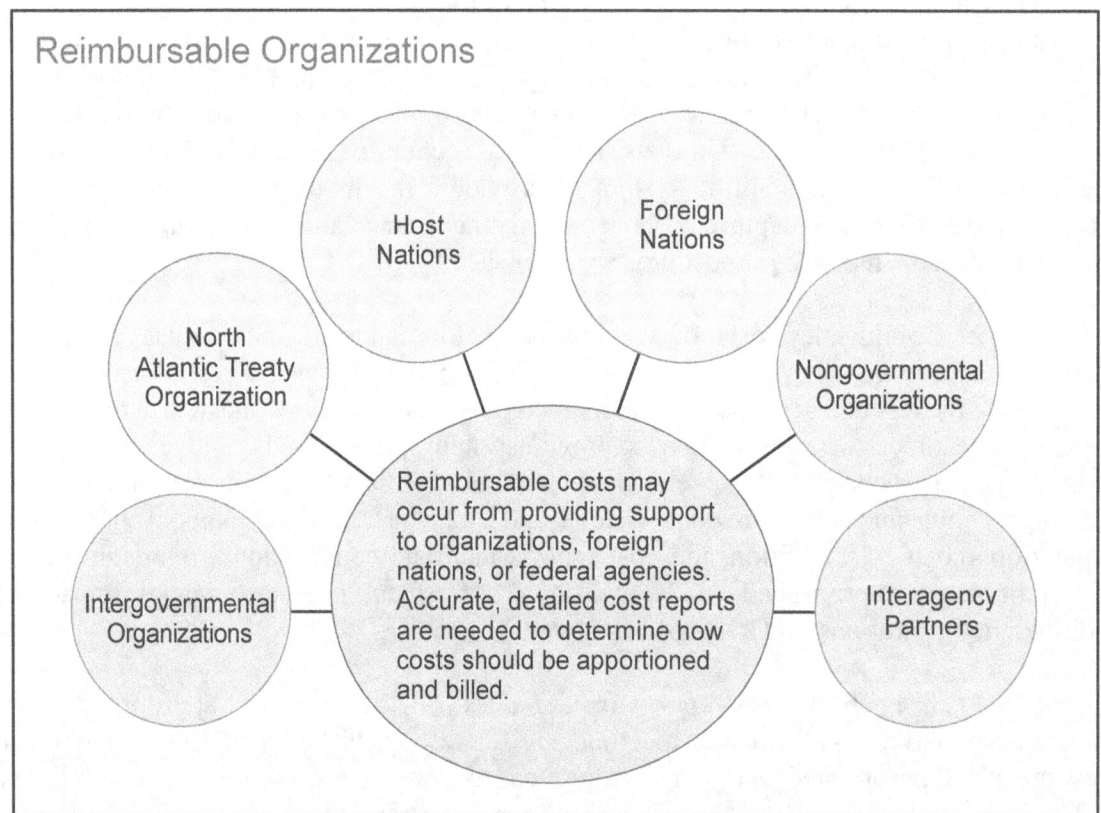

Figure III-3. Reimbursable Organizations

rendered to requesting units and agencies. If a current agreement exists, the joint force comptroller will, with legal assistance, review the agreement for proper procedures and support. If an agreement does not exist, the joint force comptroller will coordinate with the joint force J-4 and staff judge advocate (SJA) for required support.

Some of the types of authorities and agreements that may be in place are listed in Appendix E, "Financial Appropriations and Authorities," and in Appendix G, "Interagency Considerations for Financial Management."

(3) Only billable costs are submitted to USG departments and agencies, IGOs, or foreign governments in accordance with the provisions of the Foreign Assistance Act (FAA), other US laws, and the requirements of the organization being billed. Billing information provided by component commanders will include documentation as required by applicable agreements. The joint force comptroller may provide specific guidance for costs incurred that are reimbursable by another USG department or agency, foreign government, NGOs, or IGOs. Given the legal restrictions on the use of reimbursed expenses and to ensure timely recoupment of reimbursable costs to the joint force components, each DOD component must closely follow contingency operations billing procedures.

See Appendix F, "Multinational Considerations for Financial Management," for a detailed discussion of financial support to multinational operations.

(a) **Noncombatant Evacuation Operation (NEO).** Reimbursement procedures for a NEO will be accomplished in accordance with memorandum of agreement (MOA) between DOS and DOD. Contact USD(C/CFO) or Service comptrollers for provisions of existing MOAs.

(b) **UN Reimbursement Procedures.** For UN operations, reimbursements fall into one of four categories: UN determined costs, invoiced costs, letters of assist (LOAs), and leases.

1. **UN Determined Costs.** Reimbursement for these costs is accomplished at the DOD level. The JFC should ensure that accurate personnel figures are reported to the UN HQ in-theater and included on monthly cost reports submitted to DFAS. These personnel counts form the basis for reimbursement calculations.

2. **Invoiced Costs.** Requests for reimbursement for invoiced costs will be prepared by the resource manager, based upon cost reports. The resource manager should ensure that auditable documentation is available to validate and substantiate amounts reported on the cost reports. In most cases, only the incremental amount is billable to the UN (for additional information, refer to DODFMR, Volume 12, *Special Accounts, Funds, and Programs,* Chapter 23, "Contingency Operations").

3. **Letter of Assist Costs.** An LOA authorizes a government to provide goods or services to a peacekeeping operation, subject to reimbursement by the UN. Reimbursement for LOA costs is accomplished using a Voucher for Transfers Between

Appropriations and/or Funds (Standard Form [SF] 1080). Resource managers should prepare an SF 1080 voucher for the cost of the goods or services provided and reference the LOA number. All LOAs must be forwarded to the Defense Security Cooperation Agency (DSCA) for execution and billing procedures. Forward the voucher, with sufficient detailed documentation and the appropriate UN receipt records, through the chain of command to the UN. A UN official authorized to commit funds should validate the voucher before it is sent through US financial channels for reimbursement. This validation will expedite the processing of the bill at UN HQ in New York, NY. Timely and accurate voucher submission is essential to ensure the most efficient repayment of funds. The SF 1080 is forwarded to DFAS with supporting documentation and a certified contingency operations cost report to support the bill. All vouchers must provide adequate documentation for accountability and certification. DFAS will verify the LOA number and item for which a voucher is being submitted, summarize in a separate attachment, and forward the voucher to the US Mission to the UN for transmission to the UN. The UN will not accept a bill that exceeds the UN LOA ceiling. The joint force comptroller must notify DSCA if the billable costs will exceed the UN LOA. DSCA will then negotiate an LOA amendment or revision with the UN to allow for additional costs.

4. **Leases.** Leases of major end items, and the associated foreign military sales (FMS) support cases, will be managed by the DSCA. Development of leases for DOD equipment will follow normal procedures in DOD 5105.38-M, Security Assistance Management Manual, Chapter 12, "Humanitarian Assistance and Mine Action Programs," which are governed by the Arms Export Control Act (AECA).

(c) NATO Reimbursement Procedures

1. **Support Arrangements with NATO.** The NATO command HQ will sometimes require specialized logistic support from one or more of the contributing nations. Such support, when included in the mission statement of requirements, is generally requested as a mission contribution on a nonreimbursable basis (e.g., provision of medical capabilities). In other instances, the NATO command HQ may request consumable supplies or other support (e.g., fuel) on a reimbursable basis. Such requests (e.g., military equipment) must originate with the NATO command and should include an advance commitment from the NATO command financial controller that reimbursement will be provided. Such costs should be invoiced to the NATO command HQ to be reimbursed by the NATO command financial controller. Submit the SF 1080 to DFAS with sufficient detailed documentation and a certified contingency operations cost report to support the request for reimbursement.

2. **Support Arrangements with Allied Nations.** NATO doctrine establishes that logistic support is a national responsibility; however, efficiencies should be sought wherever possible. Other allied nations' forces may require logistic support, which may be provided in a number of different ways. The establishment of a support agreement annex is necessary to document this type of support. During peacetime, this is generally accomplished through the FMS program. During Article 5 or non-Article 5 operations, such support may be provided under the following arrangements:

a. **Role Specialization Arrangements.** Prior to a NATO operation, the nations providing forces may mutually agree to a division of responsibility in the operational area. Such an arrangement, for example, could result in one nation establishing a field medical facility, with another nation providing an airlift capability. Ideally, the tasks should be divided such that mutual benefit and equity are apparent and supported by law. This is an extremely valuable tool, since it provides a framework for exchange of available items to support time-sensitive mission requirements. When the US is acting as role specialist nation, any support provided to another country must be provided through an authorized mechanism. Typically, this is done through acquisition and cross-servicing agreement (ACSA) transactions.

b. **Standardization Agreements (STANAGs).** NATO nations have made commitments to pursue standardization and interoperability in a number of areas. One means of achieving this is through adaptation of common technical standards and procedures, documented in STANAGs. A body of such standardization documents exists, covering functions ranging from communications procedures to refueling other nations' aircraft. Many such agreements also include standard reimbursement procedures.

c. **Direct Reimbursement.** In the absence of other suitable arrangements, the allied nations may negotiate for support subject to reimbursement procedures of the nation providing the required supplies or services.

(d) **Acquisition and Cross-Servicing Agreement.** Bilateral ACSAs exist with many allied nations and the NATO Maintenance and Supply Organization, enabling operational commanders to arrange mutual support under payment in cash (PIC), replacement in kind (RIK), or equal value exchange (EVE) procedures.

(e) **Host-Nation Support Reimbursement Procedures.** Once the HNS agreement is established, the joint force J-4 provides a detailed statement of requirements to the HN and begins the negotiations for logistic support. Specific procedures for cost capturing and billing must be negotiated with the HN. This will prevent locally negotiated agreements that may not be legal or authorized. An SF 1080 to DFAS with sufficient detailed documentation and a certified contingency operations cost report to support the request for reimbursement must be submitted.

(f) **Foreign Nation Support (FNS) Reimbursement Procedures**

1. FNS is provided to foreign forces from countries other than the country in which the contingency operation is occurring. This support is generally provided under one of three circumstances. First, support can be provided under the existing rules of a parent organization that is controlling the operation (e.g., NATO, UN). Billing procedures under these circumstances should follow standing agreements for support. Second, support may be provided if the United States and the supported country have a bilateral agreement in place prior to the operation. The United States has many of these cooperative agreements with allies. The resource manager must consult with the legal advisor or SJA for a copy of any existing bilateral agreements and follow the procedures outlined in the agreement for

reimbursement. Third, support can be provided based upon an agreement that is negotiated expressly for the operation. Any negotiated agreement for support should include billing and reimbursement instructions. The resource manager must consult with legal counsel to determine the process and approval levels applicable to the negotiation of such an agreement.

See Appendix E, "Financial Appropriations and Authorities," for a detailed discussion on several of the legal authorities for reimbursement such as the ACSA, Sections 607 and 632 of the FAA, and the Economy Act.

2. Bills prepared for support during a UN or NATO operation should follow procedures established by those organizations. Bills prepared for either standing or negotiated bilateral support agreements should be processed as set out in the agreement. The resource manager must send these bills, as required, through Service funding channels.

(g) **Assistance in Kind (AIK).** AIK is the provision of material and services for a logistic exchange of materials and services of equal value between the governments of eligible countries. These items are accountable as future reimbursements to the country that initially provides them on a gratis basis. Costs for these items have a current value that is captured as future reimbursements. The joint force comptroller will develop and implement procedures, in coordination with logistic elements, to track the value of support provided in order to ensure an equal exchange of valued materials and services throughout the multinational operation. Particular care must be taken in accounting for these authorized exchanges due to the political sensitivity inherent in multinational operations. Ideally, these in kind reimbursements should derive no monetary gain and should provide mutual benefit and equity between the participating countries. Resource managers must consult with legal counsel to ensure that the proper agreements are in place to legally support US acceptance of AIK.

(h) **NGO Reimbursement Procedures.** NGOs do not operate within the military or governmental hierarchy. However, because NGOs operate in remote areas of high risk, they may need the logistic, communication, and security support that military forces can provide. Expectations of military support (including supplies, services, and assistance) must be reviewed with the NGOs. The joint force comptroller must consult with a legal advisor or SJA to determine the JFC's authority to provide support on a reimbursable or nonreimbursable basis. Each NGO normally has some type of financial control officer. Commanders should only provide support to NGOs after they receive approval. An MOA on reimbursement between the command and the NGO is recommended. Resource managers should ensure that all supply activities, especially fuel, maintain a record of what is provided; submit bills to supported organizations as required; and, if an organization is not authorized to make payment locally, forward the documentation (signed by both organizations) through Service funding channels.

(i) **Non-DOD Departments and Agencies Reimbursement Procedures.** Congress provides DOD with funds for very specific needs. Therefore, providing support to other USG departments and agencies can be complex. When presented with such a request for support, the resource manager should consult with the legal advisor. An MOA or interagency agreement should form the basis for any reimbursable relationship with interagency partners. These agreements can be used to ensure that only authorized support is provided, and supply and service activities capture the cost of support. Bills should be compiled as required, using a manual SF 1080, through the supported agency. The SF 1080 must have a copy of the agreement with attached substantiating documents.

(j) **Defense Support of Civil Authorities (also known as Civil Support).** In cases of a defense support of civil authorities event (e.g., national disaster), a federal agency such as the Federal Emergency Management Agency may request assistance from DOD. When approved by SecDef or CCDR, the assistance will be reimbursable under the appropriate authority, usually the Economy Act or the Stafford Act. The federal agency will provide a funding document to DOD that provides reimbursable budget authority (RBA) to cover DOD expenses incurred in rendering the requested support. In the case of United States Northern Command (USNORTHCOM), the DOD comptroller has authorized the use of a defense support of civil authorities FM process to distribute, track, and manage RBA to performing DOD organizations. USNORTHCOM may task one of its components or activate an FM augmentation team to manage RBA and financially close out the federal partner's funding document. The joint force comptroller should understand the defense support of civil authorities FM process, how DOD operations are funded, and how the Services are reimbursed.

Joint Publication (JP) 3-28, Civil Support, *Appendix A, "Reimbursement for Civil Support Operations," provides additional details on cost reimbursement.*

k. **Accounting and Fiscal Validation.** Resource managers should continuously validate funding documents and recoup or cancel invalid obligations if it is evident that funds will not be executed in a timely manner to ensure funds do not revert and are lost at the end of the fiscal year.

l. **Establish Management Internal Controls.** The joint force's comptroller should coordinate internal controls throughout the joint force that will provide reasonable assurance that obligations and costs comply with applicable laws; funds and other assets are protected; and proper accounting and documentation is kept of all expenditures. These management internal controls should be established as soon as possible, but not at the expense of operational considerations.

m. **Establish a Financial Assistance Visit and Inspection Process.** The joint force comptroller is responsible for conducting FM training, FM assistance visits, and FM inspections to ensure all matters pertaining to RM are operating properly and legally. The frequency of the FM visits and/or inspections will depend upon the duration of the operation.

n. **Provide Accurate and Complete Accounting Support.** The joint force comptroller supports the Service comptroller in ensuring official accounting records are accurate, properly supported by source documentation, and resolving accounting issues in a timely manner.

Intentionally Blank

CHAPTER IV
FINANCE SUPPORT

"Financial potency determines the issues of war."

Rear Admiral Alfred T. Mahan
1905

1. Overview

a. Finance support during joint operations ensures banking and currency support for personnel payments, theater support contracting, and other special programs. It involves financial analysis and recommendations to help the JFC make the most efficient use of fiscal resources. Effective finance support provides the financial resources necessary for successful mission accomplishment. The finance support structure must not only provide the funding (cash and negotiable instruments), but must also establish expedient methods of payment, which may include electronic funds transfer (EFT).

b. The joint force comptroller checklist in Appendix B, "Joint Force Comptroller Checklist," provides an example of the resource considerations by joint operation phase.

2. Essential Elements of Finance Support

Though each contingency operation has a unique set of parameters associated with its execution, all operations involve the essential elements of finance support discussed herein.

a. **Provide Financial Advice and Recommendations.** Early and active participation by the joint force comptroller in joint operation planning is critical to successful integration of all components' finance support. The joint force comptroller must obtain and analyze the economic assessment of the operational environment and begin initial coordination with the DFAS Crisis Coordination Center. The DFAS Crisis Coordination Center will provide advice and act as the primary DFAS liaison. The joint force comptroller will recommend joint force FM policies and develop the concept of finance support outlined in the FM appendix to the joint OPLAN or OPORD. (See paragraph 3, "Assessment Tools," for suggested assessment tools.)

See Chairman of the Joint Chiefs of Staff Manual (CJCSM) 3122.03C, Joint Operation Planning and Execution System (JOPES), Volume 2, Planning Formats, *and Appendix C, "Guide to Operation Plan Development," for a guide to preparing the FM appendix.*

(1) In order to provide the JFC with an accurate and complete FM guidance recommendation, the joint force comptroller must analyze the economic systems in the operational area, determine the impact of a joint operation on those systems, and predict the ability of the economic systems to support operations. To obtain needed information, the joint force comptroller should coordinate with the intelligence directorate of a joint staff (J-2), J-4, and civil-military operations (CMO)/civil affairs organizations to ensure that requests for information are forwarded to appropriate sources. Other sources of information

available to the joint force comptroller include the DOS, local embassy, Department of the Treasury, Department of Commerce, and Central Intelligence Agency (CIA) World Factbook country reports.

(2) The analysis includes, but is not limited to, how well the infrastructure in the JOA can support logistic and banking operations; how US currency would affect the economic system; and which currencies or scrip should be used. Effective use of the support available from sources in the JOA is an important factor in the successful sustainment of joint forces. Procurement of additional labor, materials, food, lodging, sanitation, and other services available in the JOA allows for scarce strategic lift to be used for other purposes. The results of a thorough economic assessment are utilized by both resource managers and financial support personnel. Additional factors to consider in analyzing this information are listed below (see Figure IV-1).

Additional Factors in Analyzing the Economic Impact of an Operation

- Development of the economy
- Banking system
- Currency

- Prices of goods and services
- Customs and practices

Figure IV-1. Additional Factors in Analyzing the Economic Impact of an Operation

(a) **Development of the Economy.** If the economy is very rudimentary, such as a barter economy, it may provide only limited capabilities. Conversely, a highly developed, industrialized economy may be capable of providing a greater level of support.

(b) **Banking System.** Highly developed economies can provide modern banking services such as local currency, checking accounts, and automated teller machines. These banks can also provide an inexpensive source of foreign currency or US coin and currency. Cash requirements may be reduced by local acceptance of the government purchase card. It may even be possible to establish a partnering relationship to effect the payment of accounts payable through an HN bank. Access to a local electronic funds transmission network may also be possible. All of these factors may reduce the cost of providing finance support to a joint force.

(c) **Currency.** Some currencies are not readily available on the open market. This can be critical in the early stages of a covert joint operation. The availability of currency must be determined during joint operation planning. Availability of currency can have a major effect on exchange rates and lead to large discrepancies between the official and black market exchange rates. Another planning consideration is the impact of a sudden large influx of US dollars on the local economy.

(d) **Prices of Goods and Services.** Determination of fair and reasonable labor rates is essential, as skilled and unskilled labor may be needed in all phases of the joint operation. This information also should be disseminated to ordering officers in the joint force. Prices for goods also should be determined and disseminated during planning or in the initial phase of a joint operation so that ordering officers have a measure against which to judge the reasonableness of prospective procurements. Availability of this information aids control of overall joint operation costs.

(e) **Customs and practices** of the affected populace in the JOA must be considered. For example, personal checks, travelers checks, and credit cards are not acceptable in some countries.

b. **Support the Procurement Process.** Support of the logistic system and contingency contracting efforts is critical to the success of all joint operations. Component finance units, when required, will provide funds for the local purchase of goods and services. Normally, it is more economical to purchase locally than transport from a home station. A large percentage of the finance unit's effort may be directed toward execution of this function. Procurement support is divided into two areas: contracting support and commercial vendor services (CVS) support.

(1) **Contracting support** is normally conducted by a Service component's finance unit and involves the payment for contracted services and supplies. The finance unit, to the maximum extent feasible, applies the principles of electronic commerce or electronic data interchange (EDI), which includes maximizing the use of EFT payments to vendors. Because an increased demand for locally procured items will tend to inflate prices, the subordinate JFC normally establishes a JARB to manage the prioritization and allocation of funds and available commercial support.

See JP 4-10, Operational Contract Support, *for a more detailed discussion of contingency contracting.*

(2) **CVS support** is used to satisfy requirements that cannot be reasonably provided through established logistic channels. If government purchase cards are not recognized, the vendors are normally paid in cash by finance support teams and paying agents, normally in local currency. Services and supplies such as day labor, rations supplement, and construction materials are commonly paid using CVS procedures.

(3) The **fast pay procedure** is used for processing payment vouchers with special requirements. It allows payment prior to verification that supplies have been received and accepted, under limited conditions (e.g., medical supplies for direct shipment overseas). When a purchase is made using fast payment procedures, payment is made based on the supplier's submission of an invoice, which constitutes a certification that the contractor has delivered the supplies to a post office, common carrier, or point of first receipt by the government, and that it will repair, replace, or correct nonconforming items.

c. **Provide Pay Support**

(1) **US Military.** The joint force J-1 will coordinate as necessary with the Service component commanders to facilitate pay support and ensure that all Service members are

receiving financial support. Pay support includes answering pay inquiries, initiating various types of individual local payments (e.g., casual payments, travel payments), check cashing, and local currency exchange (see Figure IV-2).

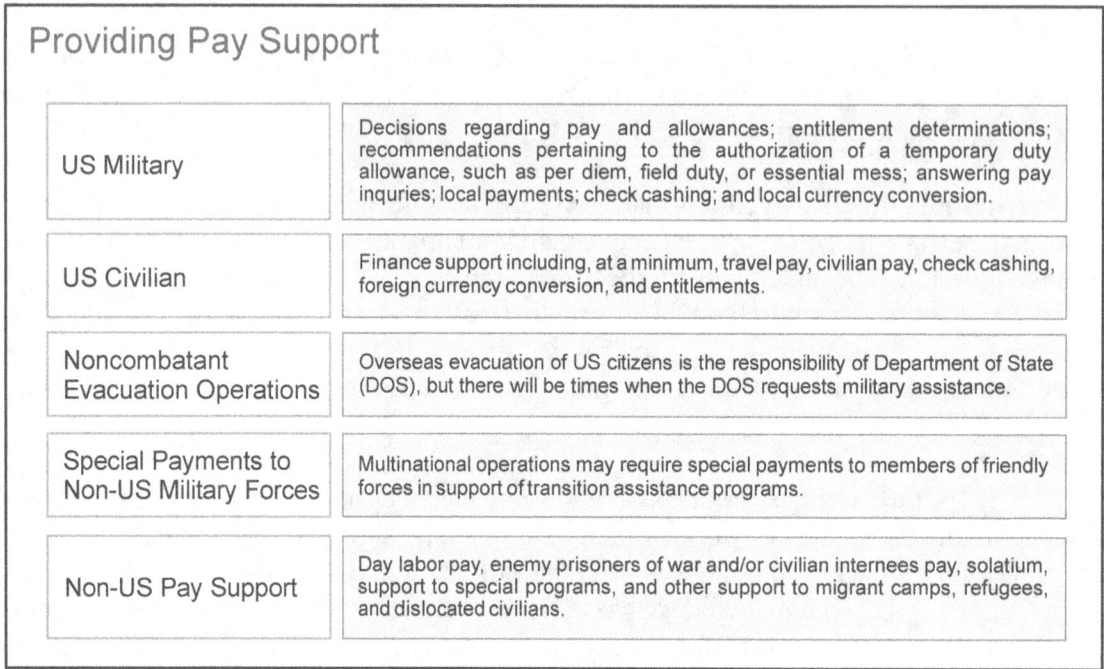

Figure IV-2. Providing Pay Support

(a) Various entitlements have been established to compensate military members for the rigors and sacrifices caused by different types of military operations. In recent years, JFCs and their staffs have become more involved in making entitlement determinations and ensuring equity among participants in joint operations. Thorough consideration of pay and entitlements issues in the early stages of joint operation planning ensures a level of consistency throughout the operation.

(b) The supported GCC's J-1, in coordination with the joint force comptroller, will make a recommendation to the GCC pertaining to Service member entitlements, including the authorization of a TDY allowance. Critical among these is the need to determine the TDY status for the initial deployment as per diem, field duty, or essential mess. The intent is to avoid situations where various Service members, serving side-by-side under similar circumstances, earn different entitlements due solely to differing determinations made by subordinate Service component commanders.

(c) Decisions made regarding pay and allowances for Service members apply equally to all components serving under similar circumstances. The JFC should announce the conditions of the operations affecting entitlements early on to ensure that deploying Service members are financially prepared. This information is particularly important as it must appear in many cases on deployment orders. Actions to request entitlements should be initiated so they are in place when the joint operation begins. Entitlement policy is a supported GCC responsibility and will be accomplished by the combatant command J-1, in accordance with the applicable DODFMR, joint Federal travel regulations (JFTR), and the entitlement matrix provided in Appendix H, "Joint Operations Entitlements and Pay Matrix."

(2) **US Civilian.** If necessary, the joint force comptroller will develop the commander's policy on finance support for USG civilians and contractors. The policy should include, at a minimum, travel pay, civilian pay, check cashing, foreign currency conversion, and entitlements as noted in Appendix H, "Joint Operations Entitlements and Pay Matrix." Eligible personnel should include contractors and their employees, US citizens who are federal employees, employees of engaged and authorized NGOs, dependents ordered to safe haven posts, and other designated civilians.

(3) **Noncombatant Evacuation Operations.** Overseas evacuations of US citizens are the responsibility of the DOS; however, there will be times when the DOS requests military assistance to execute a NEO. Based on the situation, the evacuee population may consist of nonessential military personnel, federal employees and their families, DOD family members, private US citizens, and designated foreign nationals.

(a) The NEO is a military operation, and should not be confused with the DOS-authorized or -ordered departure, which is an official order recognizing the presence of hostilities or a threat and establishing the effective "beginning date" of entitlements for official government employees and their families.

(b) The Services and DOD agencies provide funding for safe haven expenses for their respective evacuees. The Service components have the authority to provide special allowances for their Service members and family members under an authorized or ordered evacuation from an overseas location. Federal employees and their family members are also authorized pay and special allowances. Financial entitlements include, but are not limited to, advance payments (when authorized by sponsor), travel, safe haven allowances, and subsistence expense allowances to authorized individuals. The Department of State Standardized Regulation (DSSR) defines travel and safe haven entitlements for eligible federal employees and their family members. A reprint of the applicable DSSR chapter may be found in the joint travel regulations (JTR). The JFTR defines travel and safe haven entitlements for military family members. Safe haven entitlements are normally paid by the established repatriation center(s) when the safe haven is in the continental United States. If the safe haven is overseas, the geographic combatant command comptroller will coordinate entitlements with the joint reception coordination center (JRCC) in the Pentagon, through the J-8.

For more information on NEO, including the Joint Plan for DOD Noncombatant Evacuation and Repatriation and fund cites for safe haven entitlements for eligible personnel, see http://www.armyg1.army.mil/militarypersonnel/neo.asp. All regulations stated in the DODFMR Volume 12, Special Accounts, Funds, and Programs, Chapter 23, "Contingency Operations," Section 2312, "Noncombatant Evacuation Operations," should also be followed.

(c) Eligible federal employees and their families, as identified in the JTR and JFTR, are entitled to transportation to a final safe haven location or designated place at government expense. Evacuee costs borne by Service components for eligible federal employees and their families will be charged against the respective Service fund cites or submitted to DFAS for reimbursement against the respective USG department or agency in accordance with DODFMR, Volume 12, *Special Accounts, Funds, and Programs,* Chapter 23, "Contingency Operations." All other individuals must sign a promissory note to the DOS, evidencing their obligation to reimburse the USG, before boarding a military or military-chartered conveyance at the point of departure from the affected country.

(d) Any finance unit (including those at ports of debarkation) may make an advance of pay, dislocation allowance payment, and/or travel entitlement for deploying personnel supporting a NEO. The Service component commanders have the authority (Title 37, USC, Section 405a) to provide special allowances for their Service members and family members under an authorized or ordered evacuation from overseas locations. Federal employees and their family members are also authorized (Title 5, USC, Sections 5521-5527) pay and special allowances during an authorized or ordered evacuation. US citizens will receive financial assistance through the Department of Health and Human Services or the Red Cross. Payments of all authorized allowances will be provided at the repatriation site(s) used for processing evacuees. For DOD families caught in a "stop movement" due to the evacuation, toll-free numbers for each Service and USG department and agency will be provided by the JRCC. These are the only locations outside the repatriation site(s) authorized to provide separation allowances. For follow-on payments, each Service and DFAS have established central sites to support payments while the family is in a safe haven status.

(4) **Special Payments to Non-US Military Forces.** Multinational operations may require special payments to authorized members of friendly forces in support of transition assistance programs. The joint force comptroller should coordinate with joint force staff legal personnel concerning support to these and other non-US military forces. The supported GCC's comptroller must ensure that specific authority and funding is obtained from the DOD and provided to the JFC before any payments are authorized. The supported GCC's comptroller will obtain copies of such agreements and make them available to the joint force comptroller early in joint operation planning. When an agreement has been negotiated between the United States and a partner nation, US disbursing officers may be authorized to advance currency on an emergency basis to cashiers, disbursing officers, or individual members of that nation's armed forces. Such agreements may require that nation's forces to provide reciprocal support to US forces.

(5) **Non-US Pay Support**

(a) **Day Labor Pay.** HN employee and day-labor pay are provided through arrangements with the HN or by a designated component commander of the JFC. The JFC has the authority to contract HN employees for day labor and to make payments. If required, this can be delegated to contracting officers. Payment rates are determined by the DOS.

These rates, if available, should be obtained by the supported GCC and provided to the joint force comptroller during joint operation planning.

(b) **Enemy Prisoners of War (EPWs) and Civilian Internees (CIs).** The JFC is responsible for providing EPWs and CIs pay. The joint force comptroller may designate a component to provide currency and other required support. The designated component will also ensure that controls are established to process deposits to and payments from designated accounts.

(c) **Claims Payments.** Claims payments are monetary payments made by the USG for noncombat injuries or property damages. Claims are paid pursuant to the Personnel Claims Act (US personnel), Federal Torts Claims Act (US citizens), Military Claims Act (US citizens), Foreign Claims Act (FCA) (foreign personnel), or claims arising under a status-of-forces agreement. Claims will be processed and adjudicated by an area claims office or, in the case of FCA, by a foreign claims commission. The Federal Tort Claims Act will not apply in most deployments because it does not typically cover acts or omissions that occur outside the United States. As a practical matter, it will apply most often in US-based disaster operations. Claims payments can reach significant dollar amounts. The finance unit is responsible for the disbursement of, and accounting for, all claims payments.

(d) **Solatium.** A solatium payment is monetary compensation given in areas where it is culturally appropriate to alleviate grief, suffering, and anxiety resulting from injuries, death, and property loss with a monetary payment. In some societies, this payment is the culturally acceptable way of expressing sympathy to a victim or the victim's family. Prompt payment of solatia helps ensure the goodwill of local national populations, thus allowing the US to maintain positive relations with the HN. A solatium payment is made from O&M appropriations (other than claims funds) by the Military Department or DOD agency involved in an accident, regardless of the assignment of single Service claims responsibility. Payment of solatia is not an admission of liability by the United States. The GCC or, if delegated, the local commander in whose operational area the incident occurred, is responsible for determining entitlement for solatium if it is not specified in local regulations. Consult with the SJA before offering or making solatium. The finance unit, through use of paying agents, is responsible for the disbursing and accounting of all solatia.

(e) **Support to Special Programs.** DOD Rewards Program offers incentives for information and can be a remarkably effective tool in preempting enemy operations and denying sanctuary and weapons. It provides monetary, goods, or services rewards for information and other nonlethal assistance beneficial to force protection or operations against international terrorism. The program's scope is limited to specific prenominations and preapproved categories in which reward payments are restricted to instances where information leads to the capture of wanted individuals or weapons. Units may take steps to expedite the reward nomination, approval, and payment processes, but they must follow strict guidelines regardless of the procedures used.

(f) **Other Support.** Authorized mission requirements or agreements may require Service component finance sections to support occupants of migrant camps, refugees, and dislocated civilians.

d. **Provide Banking and Disbursing Support**

(1) **Functions.** Disbursing support includes, but is not necessarily limited to, making various types of payments certified as correct and proper, check cashing, and local currency conversion.

(2) **Establishment and Control of Financial Institutions.** The supported GCC, in coordination with DOS and US embassy representatives, will designate an HN banking activity with US Department of the Treasury approval. Banking support will be provided, when appropriate, by military banking facilities or the HN banking industry. When the JFC has authorized the establishment of an FM lead agent from a Service component, the FM lead agent will procure and provide US and local currency for disbursement for the joint force HQ. Each Service component will provide US and local currency for disbursement. The joint force comptroller, when required, will negotiate and provide liaison with designated HN banking institutions to establish LDAs and banking procedures. Coordination with DFAS and the US Department of the Treasury is required when negotiating with HN banking institutions; see DODFMR, Volume 5, *Disbursing Policy and Procedures,* Chapter 5, "Deposit and Transfer of Public Funds," paragraph 050102B, "General Discrepancies."

(3) **Currency Control and Support**

(a) **Currency Control.** The joint force comptroller, when required, is responsible for coordinating US and local currency procurement and control in support of the commander's requirements. The JFC may set conversion limits and policies as recommended by the US Department of the Treasury and DOS.

(b) Currency support includes supplying US currency, foreign currencies, US Treasury checks, foreign military scrip, and, in some operations, precious metals (e.g., gold, silver) to US and multinational forces. Currency and coins may also be provided to designated facilities as operational considerations permit. Finance units will exchange currency for US Treasury checks or EFT for Service members, nonappropriated fund instrumentalities, and postal units. Finance units also can provide cash for automated teller machines during joint operations. Commanders must maximize use of existing technology (to include EFT) to minimize the use of cash in the operational area. The FM lead agent should synchronize central funding locations with supported elements of all joint force components and the joint force HQ. The central funding agency must ensure that currencies are available to support finance and contracting missions for all subordinate commands and all elements not supported by assigned finance elements.

(c) **Smart Cards.** DOD utilizes several smart card applications to conduct financial transactions in a number of settings. Smart cards include stored value cards (SVCs), debit cards, and combination cards (contain both SVC and debit card features). Smart cards store or provide access to "electronic money" and provide a more secure method of handling funds. They alleviate the need to carry cash and provide electronic payment to vendors for items purchased or services rendered. Examples include the Deployed Forces Card (known as Eagle Cash) used by Service members, DOD civilians, and contractors for electronic financial transactions in overseas locations; the Navy/Marine Cash Card used aboard naval vessels; and the US Debit Card used as an alternate device for payments made by USG departments and agencies. Currently, US Treasury guidance is pending for these programs.

See DODFMR, Volume 5, Disbursing Policy and Procedures, *Chapter 17, "Smart Cards for Financial Applications," for more information.*

Intentionally Blank

APPENDIX A
FINANCIAL MANAGEMENT RESPONSIBILITIES
WITHIN THE DEPARTMENT OF DEFENSE

1. Office of the Under Secretary of Defense for Policy

The USD(P) has responsibility within DOD for certain contingency operations (peace operations, FHA, and NEOs). The USD(P) does not have responsibility for domestic disaster relief. The Assistant Secretary of Defense (Special Operations and Low-Intensity Conflict) (ASD[SO/LIC]) provides USD(P) with overall coordination of DOD activities in support of NEOs as chair of the evacuation management task force. In that capacity, the ASD(SO/LIC) ensures that existing policy and procedures for NEOs remain current, to include a memorandum of understanding with DOS.

2. Office of the Under Secretary of Defense (Comptroller)

The USD(C/CFO) is responsible for overall financial policy for contingency operations and works with USD(P) to determine the most responsive method of financing. Additionally, the USD(C/CFO) is responsible for pursuing prompt reimbursement to DOD from the UN and other multinational organizations, other nations, and interagency partners. USD(C/CFO) will coordinate with the Joint Staff J-8 to ensure that warning orders and execute orders to the CCDRs and DOD components include FM guidance. This guidance should include accounting codes established by Services and directed by USD(C/CFO) and logistic codes established by Joint Staff J-4 to track an operation's costs, billing procedures for reimbursable support, responsibilities of the supported CCDR's staff for coordination of FM issues, and any other FM instructions pertinent to the specific operation.

3. Office of the Under Secretary of Defense for Personnel and Readiness

The Under Secretary of Defense for Personnel and Readiness ensures that existing policy and procedures for NEOs are current and serves as a member of the evacuation management task force.

4. Office of the Chairman of the Joint Chiefs of Staff

The CJCS is responsible for transmitting SecDef orders to CCDRs. Whenever possible, execute orders will include a funding paragraph outlining the financial responsibilities, as directed by the USD(C/CFO) and USD(P), and a logistics annex providing organizational identification of logistic responsibility.

5. Defense Finance and Accounting Service

a. DFAS plays a critical role in support of joint operations as the DOD EA for finance and accounting. DFAS has the responsibility for DOD finance and accounting policies, procedures, standards, systems, and operations in support of the combatant commands and Services. This responsibility is exercised through the FM assistant secretaries providing direct support to the joint operation. In addition, DFAS has responsibility for centralized cost capturing of the operation for DOD and Service components.

b. To facilitate this support role, DFAS has established the Defense Finance and Accounting Support Element. Operating from the DFAS HQ Crisis Coordination Center, this organization is the single point of contact for guidance and resolution of issues. It is available to assist in the development of finance and accounting plans, policies, and procedures. In addition, this support element has the responsibility to organize DFAS activities to maximize the support provided to deployed forces. DFAS can provide liaison personnel to augment the staff of a JFC's comptroller in order to assist in establishing unique accounting requirements.

6. Services, Department of Defense Agencies, and United States Special Operations Command

a. The Services are the proponents for FM and provide guidance and implementing instructions regarding all FM issues. USSOCOM provides management and authority on use of Major Force Program-11 funding. The Services and USSOCOM allocate funds appropriated for programs established by Congress, monitor their execution, and recommend major reprogramming of funds. The heads of the DOD components are responsible for preparing cost estimates and submitting budget justifications to the USD(C/CFO), and also providing monthly incremental cost reports to DFAS in accordance with policy from the USD(C/CFO). In addition, the DOD components' HQ are responsible for providing to the DFAS, on a monthly basis, certified cost statements, supporting documentation, and completed billing documents (SF 1080 Voucher for Transfers Between Appropriations and/or Funds) for each LOA or incurred cost for which payment is requested.

b. DOD components and CCDRs can issue specific FM instructions to their subordinate activities as required to support a contingency operation. These instructions will be coordinated with USD(C/CFO) and Joint Staff J-8 to eliminate conflict. They normally include requests for cost estimates, reporting requirements, and further component-unique accounting and billing procedures.

7. Defense Security Cooperation Agency

DSCA is responsible for the management of the Overseas Humanitarian, Disaster, and Civic Aid appropriations and maintains oversight of the CCDRs' humanitarian and civic assistance (HCA) program and DOD humanitarian assistance program. The DSCA is also responsible for providing leased equipment and using FMS systems and procedures, when required, to support contingency operations. DSCA also supports the implementation of those contingency operations supported under the applicable sections of the FAA, when directed by the USD(P) to provide this support. Such support may be in response to requests from the DOS or requests from the UN for articles and services to support equipment leased under FMS procedures. The DSCA is authorized to use the FMS system network to provide such support.

8. United States Mission to the United Nations (Military Advisor)

The Office of the Military Advisor to the US mission determines the appropriate US agency to support UN requests for assistance. For the DOD, all requests should be forwarded to the USD(P) for approval and action. The Military Advisor's office will be the focal point for receipt of billings from DFAS, transmittal of information to the UN requesting offices, and follow-up to UN queries when necessary.

Intentionally Blank

APPENDIX B
JOINT FORCE COMPTROLLER CHECKLIST

1. Introduction

The joint force comptroller is the principal or special staff assistant to the JFC on FM matters. The following is a checklist, grouped by joint operation phases, of FM-related activities that the joint force comptroller should consider during joint operation planning and execution. Activities are not necessarily limited to a single phase.

2. Shape, Deter, and Seize the Initiative Phases

a. **Resource Management**

(1) Provide RM advice and assistance.

(2) Analyze all support agreements for RM implications.

(3) Ensure that the EA has been designated, when appropriate.

(4) Maintain an awareness of costs; participate in the staff estimate and joint operation planning.

(5) Perform accounting support (both appropriated and nonappropriated).

(6) Prepare appendix 3 (Finance and Disbursing) to annex E (Personnel) and review OPLANs and OPORDs to include the concept of support.

See Appendix C, "Guide to Operation Plan Development."

(7) Review RM support requirements and establishment of funding responsibility to include contracting and procurement. Ensure a mechanism is established for capturing and reporting costs.

(8) Review interagency financial support agreements.

(9) Determine if RM support is required for other activities and organizations such as morale, welfare, and recreation (MWR); public affairs; IGOs; and NGOs.

(10) In coordination with the joint force J-4, determine the availability of HNS or AIK support and establish reporting and reimbursement requirements. In coordination with the joint force J-4 and staff engineer, initiate wartime military construction requests or reprogramming actions. This includes support on ACSAs with other nations.

(11) Determine any unique reimbursement procedures through the UN, if necessary, to capture incremental costs.

(12) Request special appropriations, if required.

(13) Implement procedures to track multinational support costs and review billing procedures.

(14) Review cost estimates, when required.

(15) Coordinate with the SJA to ensure legal considerations are reviewed.

(16) Determine, if necessary, accounting and central funding support requirements.

(17) Establish management internal controls.

b. **Finance Support**

(1) Obtain and analyze consolidated economic assessments of the JOA.

(2) Provide financial advice and assistance.

(3) Determine if foreign currencies are to be used and coordinate exchange rates.

(4) Develop requirements for check cashing, emergency payments, currency conversion, funding of paying agents, foreign currency conversion, solatium, recording of cost data, travel, civilian pay, funds disbursement, and other pay support.

(5) Determine what TDY options have been designated for the operation by the JFC.

(6) Determine if group travel has been declared.

(7) Coordinate entitlement, if required, for reserve or National Guard participation.

(8) Coordinate with the joint force J-1 to ensure consistency of entitlements and level of support. If required, request determination of hostile fire pay, imminent danger pay, hardship duty pay, family separation allowance, special leave accrual, combat zone tax exclusion, and sea duty pay.

(9) Publish guidance, when required, on UN entitlements and leave for personnel assigned as observers to peacekeeping organizations.

(10) Determine check cashing limits (usually done at the local level).

(11) Coordinate with the DFAS Crisis Coordination Center.

(12) Determine banking support requirements.

(13) If required, determine appropriate quantities of foreign currencies and formalize resupply procedures.

(14) Determine and provide finance support to a NEO, if necessary.

(15) Provide, if necessary, currency funding support to other US and allied organizations in the JOA.

(16) Coordinate the LDA establishment in an HN banking facility.

(17) Prepare for solatia and payments for other claims.

(18) Coordinate with the joint force SJA to ensure legal considerations are reviewed.

3. Dominate Phase

a. Resource Management

(1) Coordinate the FM aspects of HNS and AIK.

(2) Capture costs, when required.

(3) Provide reports, as required, including those needed for reimbursement by an HN, foreign nations, IGOs, NGOs, or other government agencies.

(4) Coordinate with the joint force SJA to ensure legal considerations are reviewed.

b. Finance Support

(1) Perform, if necessary, central funding (both appropriated and nonappropriated) support.

(2) Support contracting and local procurement requirements.

(3) Control currency.

(4) Provide, if necessary, EPW or CI pay support.

(5) Provide for NEO requirements, if necessary.

(6) Provide limited pay support to joint and multinational forces and designated civilians, when authorized.

(7) Coordinate with the joint force SJA to ensure legal considerations are reviewed.

4. Stabilize and Enable Civil Authority Phases

a. **Resource Management**

(1) Identify additional sources of funds to aid sustainment of the joint operation.

(2) Obtain MWR funds.

(3) Determine requirements, when necessary, for civic assistance funding.

(4) Coordinate with the joint force SJA to ensure legal considerations are reviewed.

b. **Finance Support**

(1) Provide banking and currency support.

(2) Provide limited pay support to joint and multinational forces and designated civilians, when authorized.

(3) Provide local procurement or CVS support.

(4) Establish pay support procedures for remaining forces in the JOA.

(5) Coordinate with the joint force SJA to ensure legal considerations are reviewed.

c. **Redeployment**

(1) Coordinate and develop FM requirements to support redeployment.

(2) Close out contingency operation funding support, to include any open LDA accounts, and conduct hand-off activities with the designated military or civilian authority.

APPENDIX C
GUIDE TO OPERATION PLAN DEVELOPMENT

1. General

This appendix serves as a guide for developing the FM staff estimate during comparison of COAs as well as developing the FM appendix to an OPLAN.

2. Procedures

a. Staff estimates are central to formulating and updating military action to meet the requirements of any situation. The exact format and level of detail may vary somewhat among joint commands and primary staff sections based on theater-specific requirements and other factors. Refer to Appendix C, "Staff Estimates," of JP 5-0, *Joint Operation Planning*, and Enclosure T (Planning Development Formats) of CJCSM 3122.01A, *Joint Operation Planning and Execution System (JOPES)*, Volume 1, *Planning Policies and Procedures*, for preparing the staff estimate.

b. The FM appendix will be developed in conjunction with the joint operation planning process using the COA taken from the commander's estimate. Subordinate command FM tasks should be described and defined in sufficient detail to ensure that FM provisions are made to support all mission essential tasks. CJCSM 3122.03C, *Joint Operation Planning and Execution System (JOPES)*, Volume 2, *Planning Formats*, provides the specific format and content for annexes and appendices to an OPLAN.

c. The remainder of this appendix provides a sample template that highlights the FM considerations that must be addressed in appendix 3 (Finance and Disbursing) to annex E (Personnel) of the supported commander's OPLAN. Note: The template that follows is based on the JOPES Volume 2 format, which does not give equal importance to FM and RM. Comptrollers should ensure RM functions are sufficiently covered in paragraph 3.a.(16).

CLASSIFICATION

HEADQUARTERS

DATE

APPENDIX 3 TO ANNEX E TO XXXXX OPLAN XXXX-XX

REFERENCES: List documents essential to this appendix.

1.   Situation

a. **Enemy.** Refer to Annex B, "Intelligence." Assess the impact of enemy capabilities and probable COAs on FM support.

b. **Friendly.** List the component FM organizations and the specific tasks assigned to each supporting the FM operations of the plan. Summarize their capabilities. Include non-US military forces and US civilian agencies, such as banking institutions or embassies, that may support assigned forces in the provision of FM support (or may themselves require support).

c. **Assumptions.** State realistic assumptions and consider the effect of current operations on FM functions. These could be similar assumptions used by the GCC/subordinate JFC and Service components when developing cost estimates for the operation.

2. **Mission.** State in a clear concise statement the FM mission in support of the joint operation mission.

3. **Execution**

a. **Concept of Operations.** Summarize the intended COA and state the general concept for finance and disbursing (financial management) support in the operational area. In separate numbered subparagraphs, provide specific guidance on the following, as applicable:

(1) Funding; establishment of local depository accounts, etc.

(2) Support of contracting efforts; commercial accounts/vendor services.

(3) Military (including active duty, National Guard, and reservists) and civilian pay and allowances policies should specifically address TDY/subsistence determination under which personnel will perform duty. [Note: Entitlement information should be communicated to Service component financial managers and DFAS as soon as possible; this information is critical to accurate payment of deploying personnel.]

(4) Foreign national pay.

(5) Finance service support policies; e.g., currency conversion, check cashing, casual (local) payment, Class A agents.

(6) Support of NEOs.

(7) Pay support to day laborers.

(8) Pay support augmentation to EPWs and CIs.

(9) Currency and credit controls.

(10) Accounting, cost capture, and reporting.

(11) Inspection and audit.

(12) Internal control.

(13) Financial institutions.

(14) Physical security of cash and negotiable instruments.

(15) Solatium and other claims payment support.

(16) RM: sources of funding, coordination of contracts, RM reporting requirements, and spending plans.

b. **Tasks.** In separate numbered subparagraphs, address unique tasks required of the components to accomplish the joint FM mission.

c. **Coordinating Instructions.** This subparagraph will include, but need not be limited to, the following:

(1) Items common to two or more subordinate commands and any unique FM relationships.

(2) Coordination with adjacent commands and civilian agencies, including US diplomatic missions.

(3) Agreements with the HN, multinational forces, interagency partners, and NGOs.

4.   **Administration and Logistics.** Provide FM guidance for furnishing logistic and administrative support. As appropriate, include guidance on the following:

a. Finance and disbursing processing locations.

b. Logistic support relationships.

c. Reporting requirements.

d. Identification of any particular personnel or augmentation requirements.

e. Coordination with GCC's/subordinate JFC's J-2 to determine the point in time after which all FM plans and budgets can be declassified, if declassification is not identified in the basic plan.

5.   Command and Control

a. **Command Relationships.** Delineate pertinent command relationships.

b. **Communications System.** Discuss communications system requirements for FM support.

APPENDIX D
LEGAL CONSIDERATIONS FOR FINANCIAL MANAGEMENT

1. Introduction

This appendix provides background on several important laws that provide the basis for FM functions. It is not meant to be all-inclusive or a source of legal guidance. Financial managers who have questions regarding the legality of obligations or payments should contact their supporting SJA or legal advisor.

2. Fiscal Law

a. **General.** Of primary concern to financial managers is fiscal law. Failure to apply fiscal law principles properly may lead to unauthorized obligations or expenditures of funds and consequent administrative or criminal sanctions against those responsible. The authority to obligate USG funds is derived from Congress. The law of federal appropriations has constitutional and statutory aspects that generally identify clear rules that the Government Accountability Office (GAO) and other agencies apply to fiscal decisions. Once Congress has passed an appropriation and the President has signed it into law, agencies must request an apportionment from the Department of the Treasury within 10 days, and the Office of Management and Budget (OMB) must make apportionment within 30 days after signature. Once OMB apportions funds to DOD, DOD then subapportions funds to the military Services, USSOCOM, or DOD agencies to allocate to major commands, which in turn allot funds to subordinate units. The apportionment process must be complete before funds can be committed or obligated.

b. **USG departments and agencies require congressional appropriation to operate.** In some cases, an authorization also must be enacted before an appropriation can be obligated. An appropriation is a law passed by Congress and signed by the President, which provides budget authority for the stated purposes. No other statutes and resolutions passed by Congress, including budget resolutions and authorization acts, authorize commitment or obligation of USG funds, or withdrawal of money from the US Treasury.

c. **Budget authority** is the authorization to incur a legal obligation to pay a sum of money from the US Treasury. Budget authority is not money; it is the authority to spend money that has been appropriated. The US Treasury actually disburses cash only after an agency requests (or, in the case of DOD, issues) an EFT or a check to withdraw money from the US Treasury to liquidate an obligation.

d. **Commitments** are administrative reservations of funds, based upon firm procurement directives, orders, or requests, that authorize the creation of obligations without further approval by the official responsible for certifying the availability of funds. Issuing a commitment that authorizes an obligation in excess of an appropriation or formal subdivision of funds could result in a violation of the Antideficiency Act (see paragraph 3, "United States Code").

e. **Obligations** are amounts of orders placed, contracts awarded, services received, or similar transactions made which legally bind the USG to make payments. Congress has imposed fiscal controls which limit the ability of the Executive Branch to obligate and expend appropriated funds. Funds may be obligated only for the purposes for which they were appropriated; further, they may only be used to satisfy the bona fide needs of the fiscal year for which the appropriations are valid. In most cases, they may not be obligated beyond their period of availability. No one may obligate funds in excess of (or in advance of) an appropriation, an apportionment, or a formal subdivision of funds without specific statutory authority. If administrative lead time requires contract award prior to the receipt of funds, execute contracts "subject to the availability of funds" to ensure timely delivery of the goods or services. If this clause is used, accept no services or supplies until after receipt of funds.

f. A corollary to the purpose and bona fide needs requirements regarding obligation of funds is the general prohibition against augmentation. **Transfers from one appropriation to another are prohibited except as authorized by law.** Appropriated funds designated for a general purpose may not be used to pay for an effort for which Congress has specifically appropriated other funds.

g. **Continuing resolution authority (CRA)** is an interim legislation enacted by Congress to provide authority to specific ongoing activities where the normal fiscal year appropriation has not been enacted by the beginning of the fiscal year or the expiration of the previous CRA, pending the annual appropriation enactment by Congress. CRA authorizes continuation of normal operations at a rate not to exceed the latest congressional action or the previous year's rate. CRA does not authorize new starts or expansions to a program. A funding gap may occur in the absence of either an appropriations act or a CRA, or when the President vetoes a duly passed appropriations bill or continuing resolution following expiration of either of their predecessors. The Attorney General has determined that, absent an appropriation or a CRA, executive agencies must take immediate steps to cease normal operations. Disbursements supporting new fiscal year obligations may not be made during a funding gap unless specifically authorized by the USD(C/CFO).

3. **United States Code**

a. **The Antideficiency Act of 1870 (as amended)**

(1) The Antideficiency Act is codified in Title 31, USC, Sections 1301, 1341, 1342, 1344, and 1511-1517. It is implemented by OMB Circular A-11, *Preparation, Submission, and Execution of the Budget*; DOD 7000.14-R, *Department of Defense Financial Management Regulation*, Volume 14, *Administrative Control of Funds and Antideficiency Act Violations*. Title 31, USC, contains the basic statutory requirements for the use, control, and accounting of public funds. Title 31, USC, Section 1301, imposes the requirement to use appropriated funds only for their intended purpose(s); Section 1341 outlines limitations on expending and obligating amounts; Section 1512 outlines apportionments and reserves; and Section 1517 outlines prohibited obligations and expenditures.

(2) DODFMR, Volume 14, *Administrative Control of Funds and Antideficiency Act Violations,* states that an officer or employee may not make or authorize an obligation or expenditure that exceeds an amount available in an appropriation or formal subdivisions of funds. The GAO has determined that this statute prohibits obligations in excess of appropriated amounts and obligations that violate statutory restrictions or other limitations on obligations or spending. Officers or employees who authorize or make prohibited obligations or expenditures are subject to criminal sanctions and administrative discipline, including suspension without pay and removal from office. Good faith or mistake of fact does not relieve an individual from responsibility for a violation.

b. **The Feed and Forage Act of 1861**

(1) Title 41, USC, Section 11 (also known as the Feed and Forage Act), permits DOD to incur obligations in excess of, or in advance of, available appropriations to ensure necessary funding to support members of the Armed Forces of the United States conducting military operations.

(2) Although authority to act under the Feed and Forage Act is granted to DOD, forward-deployed units must be prepared to request urgent obligation authority during contingency operations. Units will submit requests through command RM channels.

Additional information on relevant USC authorities is contained in Appendix E, "Financial Appropriations and Authorities."

c. **Special Operations Forces Training with Friendly Foreign Forces.** Title 10, USC, Section 2011, authorizes the Commander, USSOCOM, and the commander of any other unified or specified combatant command to pay, or authorize payment for, any of the following expenses:

(1) Expenses of training special operations forces assigned to that command in conjunction with training, and training with, armed forces and other security forces of a friendly foreign country.

(2) Expenses of deploying such special operations forces for that training.

(3) In the case of training in conjunction with a friendly developing country, the incremental expenses incurred by that country as the direct result of such training.

d. **International Disaster Assistance.** Title 22, USC, Sections 2292 and 2292a, authorizes that in addition to amounts otherwise available to carry out international development up to $50,000,000 in any fiscal year may be obligated against these appropriations to furnish assistance to any foreign country, international organization, or private voluntary organization, on such terms and conditions as the President may determine, for international disaster relief and rehabilitation, including assistance relating to disaster preparedness, and to the prediction of, and contingency planning for, natural disasters abroad. The assistance provided by the US shall, to the greatest extent possible, reach those most in need of relief and rehabilitation as a result of natural and man-made disasters.

4. Law of War

The law of war addresses a wide variety of areas, including monetary issues pertaining to EPWs. Actions regarding the treatment of EPWs, from what to do with money that EPWs are carrying to how much and when to pay them for their labor, are covered within the law of war.

Additional information on payments to EPWs is contained in Chapter IV, "Finance Support."

5. Chief Financial Officers Act of 1990

a. The 1990 Chief Financial Officers Act established a centralized FM structure within the OMB and in major departments and agencies.

b. It strengthened FM internal controls by requiring the following:

(1) Preparation of an FM systems improvement plan, both government-wide and in the 23 agencies covered by the act.

(2) Preparation of audited financial statements and audits of selected activities of USG departments and agencies to hold agency heads accountable for their operations.

(3) Reporting to the President and Congress on the annual status of general and FM in the USG.

6. Federal Managers' Financial Integrity Act of 1982

The Federal Managers' Financial Integrity Act was enacted in September 1982 to strengthen internal control and accounting systems throughout the federal government and to help reduce fraud, waste and abuse, and misappropriation of federal funds. The act holds USG department and agency managers accountable for correcting noted deficiencies and requires that USG departments and agencies annually identify and report internal control and accounting system problems and planned remedies.

7. Government Management Reform Act of 1994 and the Federal Financial Management Act of 1994

The Government Management Reform Act and the Federal Financial Management Act were enacted to provide a more effective, efficient, and responsible government. These acts mandate statutory requirements for reports to Congress, the use of EFTs for payments, the establishment of a franchise fund in each of six executive agencies, and the submission of annual audited financial statements to the OMB Director.

8. Financial Management in Multinational Operations

Financial managers must be aware of the legal ramifications of operating in a multinational environment. Reimbursement and other funding issues often are complex, requiring knowledgeable financial managers.

In addition to the specific agreements governing each operation, important references on multinational funding issues are contained in DOD 7000.14-R, DODFMR, Volume 15, Security Assistance Policy and Procedures, and in this publication at Appendix F, "Multinational Considerations for Financial Management."

For additional information, see the following Web sites:
http://www.dod.mil/comptroller/
http://www.whitehouse.gov/omb/circulars/
http://www.defenselink.mil/comptroller/fmr/
http://hqinet001.hqmc.usmc.mil/p&r/
http://www.donhq.navy.mil/AAUSN/sp/ORF/ORF.htm

Intentionally Blank

APPENDIX E
FINANCIAL APPROPRIATIONS AND AUTHORITIES

1. Introduction

This appendix describes DOD and non-DOD authorities, procedures, and sources of funds that have been utilized to support a variety of joint operations. Some of the more important agreements, useful to a complete understanding of FM in joint and multinational operations, are also discussed. This appendix provides only an overview; in most cases, financial managers, along with their appropriate legal advisors, will want to consult the proper USC section, regulation, or directive prior to any expenditure of resources.

2. Department of Defense Appropriations

a. **Operation and Maintenance Appropriations**

(1) **Purpose.** These appropriations pay for the day-to-day expenses of DOD components in garrison, as well as during exercises, deployments, and military operations. However, there are threshold dollar limitations for certain types of expenditures such as purchases of major end items of equipment and construction of permanent facilities. Once expended, O&M accounts may be replenished for specific operations through supplemental appropriations from Congress, reprogramming actions, or the UN.

(2) **Procedures.** CJCS provides an execute order to a supported CCDR describing mission requirements. Normally, the supported and supporting CCDRs' Service components will fund their participation in an operation with O&M funds for mission-essential activities. However, other appropriations may be used as dictated by the mission.

(3) **Construction.** O&M funds may be used for unspecified minor military construction under Title 10, USC, Section 2805(c). The project limit is $750,000, or up to $1.5 million (M), if intended solely to correct a deficiency that is life-, health-, or safety-threatening. Also, since fiscal year 2004, Congress has authorized the use of unspecified Service O&M funds for combat and contingency related construction, which is distinct from the authority under Title 10, USC, Section 2805(c). Consult the current Military Construction Appropriation Act for limits on the use of these funds. O&M funds may also be used via the contingency construction authority with SecDef approval when specifically authorized by Congress as identified in a current national defense authorization act.

b. **Military Construction (MILCON) Appropriations**

(1) **Purpose.** Congressional oversight of MILCON is extensive. Specific approval is required for any project above an established dollar threshold. Funds for these large construction projects require specific Congressional approval and are provided in the annual Specified Military Construction Program. MILCON appropriations also fund part of the Unspecified Minor Military Construction Program. The Secretary concerned, under the authority of Title 10, USC, Section 2805(a), may use minor MILCON funds for minor projects not specifically approved by Congress. This authority is limited to projects within

prescribed dollar threshold limits. MILCON funds may be used for unspecified minor military construction projects equal to or less than $2M, or the sum of $3M or less if intended solely to correct a deficiency that is life-threatening, health-threatening, or safety-threatening. Maintenance and repair are not considered construction, and expenditure of O&M for these purposes is not subject to the construction expenditure limitation. Maintenance is recurrent work to prevent deterioration and to maintain a facility in usable condition. Repair is the restoration of a facility in order that it may be used for its original purpose. When construction and maintenance or repair are performed together as an integrated project, each type of work is funded separately, unless the work is so integrated that separation of construction from maintenance or repair is not possible. In such cases, all work is funded as construction.

(2) SecDef may undertake MILCON projects and may authorize the Secretaries of the Military Departments to undertake MILCON projects not otherwise authorized by law that are necessary to support use of the Armed Forces in cases of declaration of war or national emergency. Such projects are funded with unobligated MILCON or family housing appropriations. See Title 10, USC, Sections 2803, 2804, and 2808.

3. Department of Defense Authorities

a. Traditional Combatant Commander Activity (TCA) Funding

(1) **Purpose.** These funds are intended for use by the CCDRs to promote regional security and other US national security goals. These funds fulfill the CCDRs' need for flexible resources to interact with the militaries in their AOR, promote regional security, and other national security goals. TCA funds are not intended to replace or duplicate any other specifically authorized appropriated fund sources available to the CCDRs. Services provide this funding with both O&M and military personnel appropriations.

(2) **Procedures.** CCDRs are responsible for direct oversight and execution of traditional activities within established policy and legal guidelines. DOD and appropriate interagency working groups exercise broad review and policy oversight.

(3) **Examples.** Some examples of the use of TCA funding include military liaison teams, traveling contact teams, state partnership programs, regional conferences and seminars, unit exchanges, staff assistance and assessment visits, joint and combined exercise observers, and bilateral staff talks.

b. CCIF, Title 10, USC, Section 166a

(1) **Purpose.** The CCIF provides CCDRs with funds to support unprogrammed new emergent requirements that occur during the fiscal year. Funds may be used among other purposes for command and control (C2), joint exercises, HCA, military education and training to military and related civilian personnel of foreign countries, personnel expenses of defense personnel participating in bilateral or regional cooperation programs, and force protection.

(2) **Procedures.** The CCDR requests CJCS to provide funds for a specific purpose.

For further details, see Chairman of the Joint Chiefs of Staff Instruction (CJCSI) 7401.01, Combatant Commander Initiative Fund.

c. **Humanitarian Assistance, Title 10, USC, Section 2561**

(1) **Purpose.** This provision authorizes appropriated funds to be used to transport USG-procured humanitarian relief supplies and for other authorized humanitarian purposes worldwide.

(2) **Procedures.** To the extent that funds are authorized and appropriated for humanitarian assistance purposes, DOD funds can be used for military or commercial transportation. Currently, the DSCA manages these funds, which are contained in the overseas humanitarian, disaster, and civic aid account. Requests should be forwarded by the supported CCDR to the Joint Staff for review and approval by DSCA and ASD(SO/LIC).

d. **Transportation of Humanitarian Relief Supplies to Foreign Countries, Title 10, USC, Section 402**

(1) **Purpose.** This legal authority provides for the military transportation of nongovernmental, privately donated humanitarian relief supplies, subject to certain conditions. Assistance under this section is commonly referred to as the "Denton Program" and is jointly administered by United States Agency for International Development (USAID), DOS, and DOD.

(2) **Procedures.** DOD is authorized to transport donated supplies from NGOs and IGOs intended for humanitarian assistance purposes. This transportation is authorized without charge but on a space-available basis. Before supplies can be transported, DOD must determine their transportation is consistent with US foreign policy; they are suitable for humanitarian purposes and in usable condition; a legitimate humanitarian need exists for them by the people for whom they are intended; they will be used for humanitarian purposes; and adequate arrangements have been made for their distribution in the destination country by the NGO or IGO. DSCA manages the program and the funds. Requests should be forwarded by the supported CCDR to the Joint Staff for approval by DSCA.

e. **Humanitarian and Civic Assistance Provided in Conjunction with Military Operations, Title 10, USC, Section 401**

(1) **Purpose.** This provision of law allows the Service components to carry out HCA activities abroad. Projects must promote US and HN security interests as well as enhance readiness skills of the US forces that participate. These projects are to be conducted in conjunction with authorized military operations and can complement, but not duplicate, other assistance provided by the USG. HCA is confined to four general areas which are defined by statute: medical, dental, surgical, and veterinary care provided in rural or underserved areas of a country, including education, training, and technical assistance related to the care provided; construction of rudimentary surface transportation systems; well drilling and construction of basic sanitation facilities; and rudimentary construction and repair of public facilities. HCA projects cannot benefit any individual or organization engaged in military or paramilitary activity.

(2) **Procedures.** HCA projects must be approved by the HN government and must be supported by the US embassy, DOS, USAID, and DOD. Section 401 activities are funded from the Services' operations and maintenance accounts. ASD(SO/LIC) provides oversight within DOD.

(3) Unless expressly authorized in an appropriations act, the Defense Health Program (DHP) appropriation may not be used to fund HCA activities. The purpose of the DHP appropriation is to create and maintain high morale in the uniformed services by providing an improved and uniform program of medical and dental care for members and certain former members of those services, and for their dependents (Title 10, USC, Section 1071). Further, sums appropriated to the DHP account may be obligated or expended for purposes of conducting programs and activities under Title 10, USC, Chapter 55. From time to time, Congress will authorize limited DHP amounts be expended on specific HCA efforts.

f. **Emergency and Extraordinary Expense (EEE) Authority, Title 10, USC, Section 127**

(1) **Purpose.** This provision authorizes SecDef and Secretaries of the Military Departments to provide for any EEEs which cannot be anticipated or classified. These are designated as EEE funds within the O&M appropriation. Each Secretary of a Military Department has different amounts, depending on previously established needs. EEE funds are funds that may be used to support certain unique requirements of operations. DOD and Service regulations that cover these funds define the types of acceptable expenditures.

(2) **Procedures.** These funds are very limited in amount and are approved on a case-by-case basis. Regulatory controls apply to prevent abuse, including congressional notification requirements. The JFC or JTF comptroller may request funds through the cognizant CCDR. The CCDR may provide the requested funds or request a Service component commander provide the funds. If EEE funds are available and no other funds are appropriate to resource an essential activity, then the Service component commander normally will request approval of the Military Department Secretary through the Service HQ. This authority does not provide cash or foreign currency to conduct an activity. Rather, EEE funds provide the capability to obligate Service funds for an activity normally not authorized by O&M funding. If foreign currency is required to perform the activity, the Service finance officer must be notified to obtain the appropriate currency.

(3) **Official Representation Funds**

(a) **Purpose.** Occasionally, there will be requirements for supporting foreign military forces at official functions. Examples of this are Fourth of July celebrations, changes of command, special meals, or gifts to foreign contingent commanders.

(b) **Procedures.** Service regulations or directives should be referenced regarding proper obligation and expenditure of these funds.

For further details, see DOD Instruction 7250.13, Use of Appropriated Funds for Official Representation Purposes, *and CJCSI 7201.01,* Combatant Commanders' Official Representation Funds.

g. **Acquisition and Cross-Servicing Agreements, Title 10, USC, Sections 2341-2350**

(1) **Purpose.** Under this authority, DOD, after consultation with DOS, may enter into agreements with NATO countries, NATO subsidiary bodies, other designated eligible countries, the UN, and other IGOs that provide bilateral agreements for the reimbursable mutual exchange of logistic support, supplies, and services. This authority is limited to the purchase and sale of logistic support and does not extend to major end items of equipment (e.g., trucks, weapons systems). Per Title 10, USC, Section 2350, DOD is authorized general purpose vehicles and other nonlethal items of military equipment which are not designated as significantly military equipment on the US munitions list. Examples include vehicles, communications equipment, and training aids. This authority allows DOD to acquire or transfer logistic support outside the AECA channels. This is a limited, DOD-specific authority to both acquire logistic support without resorting to commercial contracting procedures and to transfer logistic support outside of AECA channels.

(2) **Procedures.** After consulting with DOS, DOD may enter into agreements with NATO countries, NATO subsidiary bodies, and other designated eligible countries for reciprocal logistic support, supplies, and services. However, major end items are excluded. Acquisitions and transfers are on a PIC, RIK, or EVE basis. RIK or EVE must be accomplished within 12 months after the date of delivery of the logistic support, supplies, or services. After 12 months, reimbursement must be on a cash basis.

For further details, see CJCSI 2120.01, Acquisition and Cross-Servicing Agreements.

h. **Foreign Disaster Assistance, Title 10, USC, Section 404**

(1) **Purpose.** This section provides the President with the authority to direct SecDef to provide disaster assistance outside the United States to respond to man-made or natural disasters, when necessary, to prevent loss of lives or serious harm to the environment. It enables DOD to utilize its unique airlift and rapid deployment capabilities to address humanitarian problems caused by natural or man-made disasters worldwide. Assistance provided under this section may include transportation, supplies, services, and equipment.

(2) **Procedures.** This legal authority provides for the military transportation of donated humanitarian relief subject to certain conditions.

(3) **Examples.** This authority was cited to provide blankets, water, and transportation to the earthquake-stricken people in Pakistan and for tsunami relief in southeast Asia.

i. **Excess Nonlethal Supplies, Title 10, USC, Section 2557**

(1) **Purpose.** This makes excess nonlethal DOD supplies available for humanitarian relief purposes.

(2) **Procedures.** DOD shall transfer excess nonlethal supplies to DOS for distribution.

(3) **Examples.** This authority could be cited to transfer medical supplies, meals ready to eat, and equipment in support of a humanitarian relief effort.

j. **Commanders' Emergency Response Program (CERP), Public Law 108-375, Section 1201**

(1) **Purpose.** The CERP is designed to enable local commanders in Iraq and Afghanistan to respond to urgent humanitarian relief and reconstruction requirements within their operational areas by carrying out programs that will immediately assist the indigenous population.

(2) **Procedures.** Refer to DODFMR Volume 12, Chapter 27, *Commanders' Emergency Response Program (CERP),* which implements Public Law 108-375, Section 1201, and provides detailed guidance on procedures for CERP funds. The fund is managed by the CERP Management Cell in the Office of USD(P).

k. **Additional DOD Authorities.** New public laws and changes to USC continually provide additional authorities to support DOD joint operations. Examples include coalition lift and sustainment authority provided in Public Law 109-289, Section 9008; rewards authority provided in Title 10, USC, Section 127b; and combating terrorism readiness initiative authority provided in Title 10, USC, Section 166b. The joint force comptroller should consult with appropriate Service, Office of SecDef, and legal personnel to determine which authorities are available to support the joint operation and to understand the procedures and guidance to be used.

4. United States Coast Guard Authorities

a. Per Title 14, USC, Section 476, the Commandant of the Coast Guard may expend for contingencies of the Coast Guard a sum not to exceed $50,000 in any one fiscal year.

b. The authorities, functions, and capabilities of the Coast Guard to perform its missions shall be maintained intact and without significant reduction after the transfer of the Coast Guard to the Department of Homeland Security, except as specified in subsequent acts in accordance with Title 6, USC, Section 468.

c. Whenever the Coast Guard operates as a Service under the Department of the Navy:

(1) Applicable appropriations of the Department of the Navy shall be available for the expense of the Coast Guard.

(2) Applicable appropriations of the Coast Guard shall be available for transfer to the Department of the Navy per Title 14, USC, Section 4.

5. Other Authorities

a. **Drawdown Authorities**

(1) This authority provides DOD articles, equipment, military education, and training to respond to unforseen emergencies or requirements. It can also provide DOD services. Examples include military transportation and military personnel offloading ships. This authority cannot be used for new contracting or procurement. It can be cited by DOD to contract for commercial air- or sealift if more economical. However, it cannot be used to provide housing and food under a logistic civil augmentation program contract to members of a foreign country or an IGO.

(2) There are three drawdown authorities contained within the FAA of 1961. All three require a Presidential determination and some form of notification to Congress. They are available for use within each fiscal year up to a specified dollar amount. The calculation of costs for all goods and services provided under these authorities, and reported to Congress, is on the basis of "full cost to the government." The calculation of costs includes the full cost of all military and civilian labor associated with the drawdown. Although these authorities are limited to existing defense stocks, a reduction of items from inventory below the reorder point may cause a new procurement action to replenish stocks. Such authority generally does not have funding attached. Drawdown authority does not draw a distinction between stocks that are at the retail or wholesale level.

(3) When drawdown authority is granted, there are very specific statutes that require the President to report to Congress the extent that stocks and services are drawn down. DSCA is the DOD agency responsible for reporting this information. DSCA must account for how much drawdown authority has been used and establish the reporting requirements for this type of support.

(4) Using this authority, DSCA normally directs the provision of supplies in two ways. First, DSCA may assemble a push package to be sent to the appropriate foreign contingent. Second, DSCA may direct, through an execute order, that certain stocks be provided to a specific foreign contingent.

(a) **Drawdown for an Unforeseen Emergency, FAA, Section 506(a)(1), Title 22, USC, Section 2318(a)(1)**

1. **Purpose.** Under Section 506(a)(1) of the FAA, military assistance (defense articles and defense services, and military education and training) can be furnished to a foreign country or IGO on a nonreimbursable basis due to an unforeseen emergency. It requires a Presidential determination and report in advance to Congress that an unforeseen emergency exists that cannot be met under the AECA or any other law. Peacekeeping is a recognized purpose for use of this drawdown authority.

2. **Procedures.** Normally, requests are initiated by the US embassy in the concerned country and forwarded to DOD. The CCDR also may identify needs to the plans directorate of a joint staff (J-5) for forwarding to DOS or the National Security Council. Once the concept is approved, DOS initiates documentation for the President to approve and to notify Congress. Once drawdown authority has been approved, DSCA manages the program for DOD and provides detailed accounting procedures.

(b) **Drawdown in National Interests, FAA, Section 506(a)(2), Title 22, USC, Section 2318(a)(2)**

<u>1.</u> **Purpose.** The President can drawdown DOD stocks for counterdrug, disaster relief, antiterrorism, nonproliferation assistance, and refugee and migrant assistance purposes. This authority provides articles, equipment, and military equipment and training. It can also provide DOD services. Examples include military transportation and military personnel offloading ships. This authority can be used for new contracting or procurement or it can be cited by DOD to contract for commercial air- or sealift if more economical. However, it cannot be used to provide housing and food by contract. Under this provision, the President may authorize the drawdown of articles and services for disaster relief and counterdrug purposes and for refugee and migrant assistance under the Migration and Refugee Assistance Act of 1962 (Title 22, USC, Section 2601[c][1]). It requires a Presidential determination and report, in advance, to Congress that it is in the national interest to execute the drawdown.

<u>2.</u> **Procedures.** The same as *Drawdown for an Unforeseen Emergency.*

(c) **Drawdown for Peacekeeping Operations (PKO), FAA, Section 552(c), Title 22, USC, Section 2348**

<u>1.</u> **Purpose.** The President can drawdown commodities and services from any USG department or agency for unforeseen emergencies to support peacekeeping activities. This authority can be used for new contracting or procurement and it can be cited by DOD to contract for commercial air- or sealift if more economical. However, it cannot be used to provide housing and food. It requires a Presidential determination and report, in advance, to Congress that an unforeseen emergency exists that requires the immediate provision of assistance.

<u>2.</u> **Procedures.** The same as *Drawdown for an Unforeseen Emergency.*

For additional guidance on drawdown procedures, see DOD 5105.38-M, Security Assistance Management Manual, *paragraph C11.4, and* DSCA Handbook for FAA Drawdown of Defense Articles and Services.

b. **Foreign Military Sales Authorizations, Title 22, USC, Sections 2761-2767**

(1) **Purpose.** FMS is used to sell defense articles and services to eligible IGOs and foreign governments. This is the primary authority to sell and lease defense articles and services (procured with DOD appropriations) to foreign allies, friendly nations, and IGOs.

(2) **Procedures.** The IGO or another country can enter into an FMS contract with DOD through a LOA. Ordinarily, the contracting country pays DOD in advance for all costs plus an administrative surcharge. FMS as well as ACSA are the only authorities available to DOD to lease defense articles and services. Leases are processed as standard FMS cases and are generally on a reimbursable basis. However, leases of defense articles may be made on a nonreimbursable basis if the article has passed three quarters of its normal service life.

c. **Authority to Transfer Excess Defense Articles, Title 22, USC, Section 2321j.** Excess defense articles authority provides for the sale or no-cost transfer of excess defense articles no longer needed by the DOD. Priority is given to eligible NATO countries and major non-NATO allies on the southern and southeastern flank of NATO, and to the Philippines.

d. **Economic Support Fund (ESF), FAA, Section 531, Title 22, USC, Section 2346**

(1) **Purpose.** The purpose of ESF is to furnish assistance to countries based on special economic, political, or security interests of the United States. Most ESF assistance is provided as cash grant transfers to help other countries improve their balance of payments. The remainder is spent on commodity support to import US goods for development projects. ESF shall be available for economic programs only and may not be used for military or paramilitary purposes.

(2) **Procedures.** The President is authorized to furnish assistance to countries and organizations, on such terms and conditions as may be determined, in order to promote economic or political stability. DOS usually provides funds directly to the countries involved. However, DOS can provide these funds to DOD through an agreement pursuant to the FAA, Section 632. The agreement is developed by USD(C/CFO) and their counterparts at DOS. If the GCC determines a need for these funds, the Joint Staff J-5 may be contacted.

e. **PKO Fund, FAA, Section 551, Title 22, USC, Section 2348**

(1) **Purpose.** The PKO Fund is used to furnish assistance to friendly countries and IGOs pursuant to the national interests of the United States. The President is authorized to furnish assistance to countries and organizations, on such terms and conditions as may be determined, for PKO and programs. Such assistance may include reimbursement to DOD for expenses incurred pursuant to Section 7 of the United Nations Participation Act (UNPA) (see paragraph 4h).

(2) **Procedures.** DOS usually provides funds directly to the countries involved. However, DOS can provide these funds to DOD through an agreement pursuant to FAA, Section 632. The agreement is developed by USD(C/CFO) and their counterparts at DOS. If the supported GCC determines a need for these funds, the Joint Staff J-5 may be contacted. Preferably, the Service component commander funding the operation for the GCC will contact USD(C/CFO).

f. **International Military Education and Training (IMET), FAA, Sections 541-545, Title 22, USC, Sections 2347-2347e**

(1) **Purpose.** The IMET program is a low cost, key funding component of US security assistance that provides training on a grant basis to students from allied and friendly nations. Authority for the IMET program is found pursuant to Chapter 5, part II, FAA 1961. Funding is appropriated from the International Affairs budget of the DOS. It is a key component of US security assistance that is an investment in ideas and people and has an overall positive impact on the numerous students trained under the program. For a relatively

modest investment, it presents democratic alternatives to key foreign military and civilian leaders.

(2) **Procedures.** DOS obtains a request for training from the HN government and passes the request to DOD. If the GCC desires to provide military education or training to countries in the AOR, this would usually be arranged through the country team at the embassy. The GCC also may submit the proposal to the Joint Staff J-5 for interagency review. Once approved by DOS, DOD through DSCA, will attempt to provide the services directly. If DOD is unable, then a security assistance tasking can be prepared, citing IMET funds. DSCA will then contract for the required support.

g. **Furnishing of Services and Commodities, FAA, Section 607, Title 22, USC, Section 2357**

(1) **Purpose.** This provision authorizes any USG department or agency to furnish services and commodities on an advance-of-funds or reimbursement basis to friendly countries, IGOs, the American Red Cross, and voluntary nonprofit relief agencies registered with, and approved by, the USAID.

(2) **Procedures**

(a) DOS obtains requests for commodities and services from the UN as well as other nations. After review, these requests may be forwarded through DOD Assistant Secretary of Defense (Strategy and Requirements) to DSCA for execution. Once DSCA approves shipment of the commodities, DFAS will submit a billing statement to the UN or other organization, which will then reimburse the Service. The determination required by the statute must be made each time a new operation will be supported under this authority. The authority for making this determination has been delegated to the Secretary of State and to the Administrator of USAID.

(b) Support of each new operation under Section 607 authority requires the negotiation and conclusion of a separate agreement. Section 607 agreements set the overall terms and conditions that govern the provision of assistance and have been used in UN operations in Somalia, the Former Republic of Yugoslavia, Rwanda, and Haiti. The UN LOA procedure is the ordering mechanism specified in those agreements.

(3) **Reimbursements.** Under Section 607, assistance may only be furnished on an advance-of-funds or reimbursable basis. Reimbursement cannot be waived. Reimbursements received may be deposited by the Service providing the assistance back into the appropriation originally used (or, if received within 180 days of the close of the fiscal year in which the assistance was furnished, into the current account concerned). These amounts then remain available for the purposes for which they were appropriated. Reimbursements received after this 180-day period cannot be retained by DOD and must be deposited in the miscellaneous receipts account of the general treasury.

h. **Section 7 of the UNPA, Noncombatant Assistance to United Nations, Title 22, USC, Section 287d-1**

(1) **Purpose.** This section authorizes support to UN PKO. This authority permits DOD to contribute personnel, nonlethal equipment, supplies, and services to UN operations.

(2) **Procedures.** The UN will issue an LOA to the United States Mission to the United Nations (USUN) in New York, NY. USUN forwards the LOA to DOS, where it is reviewed and transmitted to DOD with a recommendation as to approval and funding. Within DOD, the USD(P) coordinates the UN request. Upon approval, DOD will direct a Service to implement the LOA.

(3) **Reimbursements.** Reimbursement normally is required from the UN. However, reimbursement may be waived when the President finds exceptional circumstances or that such waiver is in the national interest. The DOS also has the authority to waive reimbursement after consultation with DOD.

   i. **Sections 628 and 630 of the FAA, Title 22, USC, Sections 2388 and 2390**

(1) **Purpose.** Consistent with the purposes of the FAA, Section 628, the President may authorize the head of a USG department or agency to assign an officer or employee of that agency to an IGO to serve on that organization's staff or "to render any technical, scientific, or professional advice or service" to that organization. There is no limit on the number of personnel that may be provided under this authority. This authority has been interpreted broadly and has been used as authority to provide US military members to peace enforcement operations (e.g., US logisticians in Somalia).

(2) **Reimbursements.** Reimbursements for Section 628 details are governed by Section 630 of the FAA. US policy is that DOD will be reimbursed the incremental costs associated with their participation in a UN operation.

   j. **The Economy Act (Agency Agreements, Title 31, USC, Section 1535).** This act provides general authority for interagency transactions. It authorizes interagency transactions when no other statute permits the providing agency to render the requested goods or services.

Additional information on the Economy Act is contained in Appendix G, "Interagency Considerations for Financial Management."

   k. **Stafford Disaster Relief and Emergency Assistance Act of 1988, as amended, Title 42, USC, Sections 5121-5206**

(1) **Purpose.** The Stafford Act provides for an orderly and continuing means of assistance by the USG to state and local governments in carrying out their responsibilities to alleviate disaster-related suffering and damage.

(2) **Procedures.** Upon the request of the affected state's governor, the President may declare an emergency or major disaster, thereby permitting mobilization of federal assistance under the Act. The Stafford Act requires reimbursement to DOD for the incremental costs of providing support. Approval authority and reporting requirements vary, depending on the duration and type of support requested. The President may direct any USG

department or agency to undertake missions and tasks on either a reimbursable or nonreimbursable basis.

6. Agreements

a. United Nations Letter of Assist

(1) A UN LOA is a document issued by the UN to a contributing government authorizing that government to provide goods or services to UN peacekeeping forces. An LOA typically details specifically what is to be provided by the contributing government and establishes a funding limit that cannot be exceeded. General support LOAs can be negotiated with the UN (if such LOAs are advantageous to both parties) to cover more generic categories such as subsistence, fuel, sustainment, and spare parts. More than one item or service can be included on an LOA. LOAs are considered by the UN to be contracting documents and must be signed and issued by the UN Director, Field Operations Division. The LOA is not considered a funded order, and the UN does not normally provide an advance of funds for the value of the LOA.

(2) The UN will reimburse contributing countries for the costs of their activities in accordance with UN standard procedures covered in the *United Nations Guidelines to Contributing Governments* and specific and general LOAs. The UN should approve all elements of national contributions and the extent of reimbursement prior to an actual deployment, if possible. Therefore, activities undertaken, troops deployed, or costs incurred for items and services rendered which are not agreed to in advance by the UN will not normally be reimbursed by the UN. Only expenditures in support of an operation approved by the Security Council and authorized by the General Assembly as a legitimate charge to the UN are eligible for reimbursement.

b. **Memoranda of Agreement.** An MOA is an agreement between countries or eligible organizations that delineate responsibilities among the participants. Among these responsibilities are the participants' financial liabilities for support. These agreements define the specific mechanisms required for reimbursement of costs. An example of the use of this authority is when coalition partners cooperate in a military operation. In this case, support can be provided to foreign forces with which the United States has an MOA. MOAs between DOD and the defense ministries of other nations or between DOD and IGOs must be based on specific legal authority and negotiated in accordance with proper procedures.

c. Department of State Funds (632 Agreements)

(1) **Purpose.** DOS and DOD may negotiate agreements where DOD agrees to initially fund requirements that are legally a DOS responsibility. These agreements are called "632 Agreements." They are generally negotiated for a specific purpose with a specific amount of funds attached. Once these agreements are signed, they provide the legal authority for DOD to incur obligations on a reimbursable basis for the purpose intended. The documentation will be consolidated and sent to DOS for reimbursement.

(2) **Examples.** Examples of the use of this agreement by DOD and the reimbursement by DOS include the paying of stipend payments to foreign military forces,

providing support to foreign military forces not covered under "506(a)(1) Drawdown Authority," funds to cover emergency medical evacuation of foreign soldiers to US medical facilities, and providing special dietary requirements for foreign contingents.

Intentionally Blank

APPENDIX F
MULTINATIONAL CONSIDERATIONS FOR FINANCIAL MANAGEMENT

1. General

a. Multinational operations is a collective term describing military actions conducted by forces of two or more nations, typically organized within the structure of a coalition or alliance. An **alliance** is the relationship that results from a formal agreement (e.g., treaty) between two or more nations for broad, long-term objectives that further the common interests of the members (e.g., NATO). A **coalition** is an ad hoc arrangement between two or more nations for common action (e.g., Operation IRAQI FREEDOM participating nations).

b. Financial considerations may vary greatly with each multinational operation. Many arrangements will be similar to those for UN operations as stated in paragraph 2 below. Other financial arrangements will be based on specific coalition agreements, memoranda of understanding, or technical agreements. It is important to begin coordination of financial arrangements with prospective multinational partners as early in the planning process as possible. Often, financial arrangements may be supported by special US logistic and funding authorities. Examples of unique authorities include the provision of supplies, services, transportation, and logistic support to coalition forces supporting military and stability operations in Iraq and Afghanistan (Public Law 109-289, Section 9008) and authorities to use ACSAs to lend certain military equipment to foreign forces in Iraq and Afghanistan for personnel protection and survivability (Public Law 109-364, Section 1202).

c. Military operations such as PKO and FHA have evolved alongside the traditional forms of military action exemplified by deterrence and combat. IGOs and NGOs will play an increasing role in the management of crisis response and limited contingency operations, and major operations and campaigns. The level of US participation in these operations is dependent on the objectives agreed to at the national level.

2. United Nations Mandated Operations

a. A variety of military missions may be conducted under the authority of a UN resolution or the UN Charter. Section 7 of the UNPA (i.e., US law) authorizes support to UN PKO. This authority allows DOD to contribute personnel, nonlethal equipment, supplies, and services to UN operations. Support provided to the UN under Section 7 UNPA authority does not require the negotiation of an agreement. However, there are formal agreements, such as Section 607 agreements, Section 628 agreements, and UN LOAs, established in most cases to facilitate reimbursement for services provided.

b. Any support provided to UN forces must be preapproved by a UN official authorized to commit funds. This will normally be the chief administrative officer or the chief procurement officer. Therefore, activities undertaken, troops deployed, or costs incurred for items which are not agreed to in advance by the UN (as identified and detailed in the guidelines, aides memoire, verbal or specific notes, or general LOAs) normally will not be reimbursed by the UN. Financial responsibilities normally will be included as part of the agreement between the contributing countries and the UN and will include the details of the financial responsibilities of each party. The US position is normally negotiated by DOD in coordination with DOS. Close coordination with UN officials throughout the military operation should ensure proper reimbursement for all UN-authorized expenditures.

c. Title 10, USC, Section 405, prohibits using DOD-appropriated funds to make a financial contribution directly or through another department or agency of the US to the UN for the costs of a UN peacekeeping activity. Congress has continued to include provisions in National Defense Authorization Acts that require giving 15 days prior notice to Congress before transferring any defense articles or services to another nation or IGO for use in UN peace operations or any other international peacekeeping, peace enforcement, or humanitarian assistance operation.

d. When participating in UN-mandated military operations two types of documents are critical to FM. The first are those standing agreements that are in place related to contributing country participation. These documents are general in nature and provide guidelines on what the UN is willing to pay for without any further, specifically negotiated, agreements. An early understanding of these documents is essential to ensure proper reimbursement for US participation in a UN operation. Listed below are some examples of the types of support arrangements listed in the standing UN procedures.

(1) **Predeployment Actions.** Preparation of personnel and equipment for deployment is the responsibility of the contributing country and includes all preparation costs involved to get the personnel or equipment to the point of embarkation. Billing the UN for reimbursement of these expenses will be based on advance negotiations with the UN.

(2) **Deployment and Redeployment Actions.** The UN can fund all deployment and redeployment costs. These activities may be organized by the contributing government, but the arrangements must be agreed to in advance by the UN. All transportation to be provided by the contributing country must be coordinated and approved by the UN. If reimbursement is requested, it will only be made up to the amount it would have cost the UN to accomplish the move.

(3) **Self-Sufficiency Period.** Each participating nation's force must be self-sufficient in the operational area until UN operations and control are sufficiently established to provide sustainment. Normal and agreed-to costs incurred during the self-sustainment period will be reimbursed by the UN. All deployed military units should be self-sufficient in rations; water; and petroleum, oils, and lubricants (POL) for a minimum of 30 days; and other classes of supplies for a minimum of the first 60 days after deployment.

e. The other method the UN uses to request support is through LOAs. A UN LOA details specifically what is to be provided by the contributing government and establishes a funding limit that cannot be exceeded for that specific LOA. General support LOAs can be negotiated with the UN, if such LOAs are advantageous to both parties, to cover more generic categories such as subsistence, POL, sustainment, and repair parts. LOAs are considered by the UN to be contracting documents and must be signed and issued by an authorized UN official.

f. The approved LOA is issued by the UN to the USUN, where it is acted on by the US Military Advisor, who determines the appropriate US agency to receive the request. From DOD, all requests should be forwarded to USD(P) for approval and action. The USD(P) will determine the appropriate organization and provide a copy of the LOA to that organization and DFAS. DFAS is responsible for maintaining a status of all active LOAs.

g. The LOA is not considered a funded order, and the UN does not ordinarily provide an advance of funds for the value of the request. Therefore, an LOA does not provide any additional obligation authority to accomplish the order. The Secretary of the Military Department must accomplish the requirement using existing O&M funds or other appropriated funds and prepare an SF 1080 for the cost of the goods or services provided, referencing the appropriate LOA.

h. **UN Personnel Reporting.** The UN reimburses participating countries for personnel provided. The UN pays providing countries a basic monthly rate per person for pay and allowances plus a usage factor for clothing and equipment and a supplementary payment for specialists.

3. North Atlantic Treaty Organization Operations

a. **Background.** NATO is an alliance of nations (including the United States) who have entered into a mutual defense treaty. Under Article 5 of the North Atlantic Treaty, an attack upon the territorial integrity of a member state is to be considered an attack on all member states. While mutual defense remains the primary mission of the Alliance, NATO has recently expanded its sphere of activities to include peace support missions outside the territorial boundaries of the allied nations. Such non-Article 5 operations may be undertaken upon the request of the UN with the unanimous consensus of all member states.

b. **NATO Funding Eligibility.** NATO conducts missions on the basis of force and capability contributions from its member states. Unlike the UN, it does not provide reimbursement for peacekeeping forces or in any other way underwrite the costs of national participation. As a result, NATO operating budgets are small in relation to those of national forces deploying in support of a NATO operation. NATO funding is generally restricted to establishment and support of the NATO HQ in the operational area. In exceptional circumstances, the NATO nations may fund projects which benefit both the NATO HQ and all participating nations' forces in the operational area (e.g., communications systems or certain engineering projects supporting main supply routes or ports). The NATO operational HQ may establish a multinational logistics center to coordinate this effort among the forces in the operational area.

c. **NATO Funding Sources.** The support of national forces in the operational area is a national responsibility and is funded through national systems and budgets. In the exceptional circumstance that a category of expenditure might be considered eligible for

NATO funding, the requirement must be submitted through the operational NATO HQ for inclusion in the budgetary plans described above. NATO funds its C2 structure through two primary sources.

(1) The **NATO Security Investment Program** is generally used to support major investments in operational infrastructure, such as construction or communications systems. Projects originate with the NATO operational HQ engineers and are subsequently screened by the NATO chain of command prior to being reviewed by the NATO Infrastructure Committee at NATO HQ in Brussels, Belgium. Funding is approved and provided on a project-by-project basis, and funds cannot be transferred between projects.

(2) The **NATO Military Budget** is the normal source of funding for O&M costs of supporting NATO HQ in the operational area. NATO operational HQ funding requirements are assembled by the financial controller and consolidated into an operational budget. This budget is screened by the NATO chain of command prior to submission to the Military Budget Committee, also located in Brussels, Belgium. Funding is approved in accordance with the proposed expenditure plan; however, there is generally some flexibility between budgetary line items.

d. **Centralized Contracts.** To reduce competition for resources in the operational area, the NATO HQ may solicit and consolidate operational area-wide requirements in order to negotiate basic ordering agreements with local vendors. Such agreements typically establish the prices, ordering procedures, and payment terms but do not obligate NATO or the nations to purchase specific quantities of goods or services. While allied nations are generally authorized to utilize such contracts on the same basis as the NATO operational HQ, the existence of such agreements does not preclude nations from negotiating their own bilateral contracts. NATO will not finance national requirements; such contracts call for nations to make direct payment to vendors for goods and services they order.

APPENDIX G
INTERAGENCY CONSIDERATIONS FOR FINANCIAL MANAGEMENT

1. General

a. **Purpose.** This appendix prescribes policies and procedures applicable to transactions where goods or services are procured by a USG activity from another USG activity under the Economy Act, Title 31, USC, Sections 1535 and 1536. Transactions include inter-Service, intradepartment, and interagency support; a requesting/customer activity needing supplies or services obtains them from another servicing/performing activity. Within DOD, Economy Act orders typically are executed by issuance of a Department of Defense (DD) Form 448, *Military Interdepartmental Purchase Request (MIPR)*.

b. **Non-Economy Act Orders.** In some cases, a DOD activity may use Non-Economy Act authorities such as Acquisition Services Funds or Franchise Funds to place an order for goods or services with a non-DOD agency. Such orders are not as common as Economy Act orders and also include a fee or similar cost. Therefore, this appendix focuses on orders placed under the Economy Act.

c. **Overview.** The Economy Act provides authority for a USG activity to order goods and services from another USG activity (including other Military Departments and DOD agencies) and to pay the actual costs of those goods and services. An activity within a DOD component may place an order with another activity within the same DOD component, another DOD component, or with another USG department or agency for goods or services.

d. **Legal Authority**

(1) In accordance with Title 31, USC, Section 1535, the head of a USG department or agency or major organizational unit within that agency may place an order with a major organizational unit within the same agency or another USG department or agency for goods or services if:

(a) Funds are available.

(b) The head of the requesting agency or unit decides the order is in the best interest of the USG.

(c) The agency or unit to be asked to fill the order is able to provide the ordered goods or services.

(d) The head of the agency decides that ordered goods or services cannot be provided as conveniently or economically by a commercial enterprise.

(2) Title 31, USC, Section 1536, provides for the crediting of payments from purchases between executive agencies so as to be available to replace stocks on hand, unless:

(a) Another law authorizes the amount to be credited to some other appropriation.

(b) The head of the performing agency decides that replacement is not necessary, in which case the amount received is deposited in the US Treasury as miscellaneous receipts.

(3) In accordance with Title 10, USC, Section 2205, reimbursements made to DOD appropriations under Title 31, USC, Sections 1535 and 1536, for services rendered or supplies furnished may be credited to the appropriation or fund of the activity performing the reimbursable work.

e. **Limitations.** Because of previous instances of abuse, limitations on the use of Economy Act orders have been imposed. Economy Act orders may not be used by an agency to circumvent conditions and limitations imposed on the use of funds, including extending the period of availability of the cited funds. Acquisitions under the Economy Act are subject to the requirements of Federal Acquisition Regulation (FAR) Subpart 7.3, *Contractor Versus Government Performance.* The Economy Act may not be used to make acquisitions conflicting with a USG activity's authority or responsibility. An Economy Act order cannot be used by one organizational unit to order work or services from another organizational unit under the same activity commander where the activity commander is in a position to fund the required goods or services through the use of direct funds.

2. Initiating an Economy Act Order

a. A USG department or agency or subordinate unit head may initiate an Economy Act order provided that all the conditions specified in Title 10, USC, Section 1535, are met.

b. **Determinations and Findings Requirements**

(1) In general, all Economy Act orders must be supported by determinations and findings (D&F) that the use of interagency support capabilities is in the best interest of the USG and that the required goods, supplies, or services cannot be obtained as conveniently or economically by contracting directly with a private source.

(2) Economy Act orders that require a contract action by a non-DOD servicing/providing activity also will include a statement on the D&F that supplies and services provided comply with one or more of the following provisions:

(a) The acquisition appropriately will be made under an existing contract of the servicing agency, entered into before placement of the order, to meet the requirements of the servicing agency for the same or similar goods, supplies, or services.

(b) The servicing agency has the capabilities or expertise to enter into a contract for such goods, supplies, or services which are not available within the requesting agency.

(c) The servicing/providing activity specifically is authorized by law or regulation to purchase such goods, supplies, or services on behalf of the requesting/customer activity.

c. **Inter-Service Support.** DOD activities shall render requested support to other DOD activities when the head of the requesting activity determines that it would be in the best interest of the USG, and the head of the servicing activity determines that capabilities exist to render the support without jeopardizing assigned missions. These determinations are accomplished by signing a support agreement (blocks 8 and 9 on DD Form 1144, *Support Agreement*). No further written determinations generally are required for agreements between DOD activities.

d. **Intragovernmental Support.** DOD activities may enter into support agreements with non-DOD activities when the head of the major organizational unit ordering the support determines that funding is available to pay for the support, it is in the best interests of the USG, the supplying activity is able to provide the support, the support cannot be provided as conveniently or economically by a commercial enterprise, and it does not conflict with any other agency's authority. This authority may be delegated, although designees may not be lower than senior executive service or flag or general officer levels.

3. Uses of Economy Act Orders

a. Economy Act orders may be used for any required goods, supplies, or services that are appropriate and legal, subject to the provisions of paragraphs 1, "General," 2, "Initiating an Economy Act Order," and 4, "Policy." Typical uses include, but are not limited to:

b. **Inter-Service Support Agreements.** This type of agreement typically is used for, but not limited to, base support (host-tenant) services such as administrative services, civilian personnel services, community services, environmental compliance, fire protection, food service, health service, mail service, police service, security/guard services, and warehousing. Services such as testing and evaluation, and level of effort work-years may be covered by Economy Act orders.

c. **Intragovernmental Agreements.** This includes support provided to non-DOD USG activities that is not provided pursuant to other statutory authority.

4. Policy

a. **Specific, Definite, and Certain.** Economy Act orders (inter-Service and intragovernmental support agreements) shall be specific, definite, and certain both as to the work encompassed by the order and the terms of the order itself.

b. **Certification of Availability for Purpose.** Economy Act orders are subject to the same fiscal limitations that are contained within the appropriation from which they are funded. However, the performing entity may not be aware of all such appropriation limitations. Therefore, the requesting official should provide a certification on, or attached to, the Economy Act order, that the funds cited on the Economy Act order are properly chargeable for the purposes cited in the order.

c. **Bona Fide Need.** Economy Act orders citing an annual or multiyear appropriation must serve a bona fide need arising, or existing, in the fiscal year (or years) for which the appropriation is available for obligation. Otherwise, a valid obligation is not accomplished. Bona fide need generally is a determination of the requesting activity and not that of the servicing activity. A servicing activity should, however, refuse to accept an Economy Act order if it is obvious that the order does not serve a need existing in the fiscal year for which the appropriation is available.

d. **Appropriation Policy**

(1) **Obligation.** An Economy Act order obligates the applicable appropriation of the requesting agency or unit upon acceptance of the order by the servicing agency. The requesting agency obligates the entire amount of a reimbursable order when the order is accepted.

(2) **Deobligation.** It is critical that activities reconcile the obligation status of Economy Act orders and deobligate unused funds, as needed, before the end of the funds availability. Funds must be deobligated by both the requesting and servicing agency to the extent that the servicing agency or unit filling the order has not, before the end of the period of availability of the appropriation of the requesting or ordering agency, provided the goods or services, or entered into an authorized contract with another entity to provide the requested goods or services.

e. **Commencement of Work.** The work to be performed under Economy Act orders shall be expected to begin within a reasonable time after its acceptance by the servicing DOD component or organizational unit.

f. **Contingent Event Prohibition.** Economy Act orders shall not be issued if commencement of work is contingent upon the occurrence of a future event or authorizing action by the requesting DOD component.

g. **Prohibitions.** Economy Act orders may not be used to contravene provisions of the law or to accomplish what regulations do not permit under commercial contracts. Economy Act orders may not be issued to extend the availability of appropriations.

5. **Ordering and Payment Procedures**

a. **Ordering Procedures.** An Economy Act order may be placed on any form that is acceptable to both the requesting and servicing activities involved based upon the documentation standards in DODFMR, Volume 11A, *Reimbursable Operations, Policy, and Procedures,* Chapter 1, "General Reimbursement Procedures and Documentation, paragraph 010204, Documentation Standards." Typically, between DOD components, a military interdepartmental purchase request (MIPR) is used to place the order. A DD Form 448-2,

Acceptance of MIPR, is used to show acceptance. Economy Act orders may be placed on a reimbursable or direct fund citation basis. The two parties will usually negotiate to determine the funding citation. An Economy Act order should include:

(1) A description of the supplies or services ordered.

(2) Delivery requirements.

(3) A funds citation (either direct or reimbursable).

(4) A payment provision which may include the citation of the account number associated with a DOD purchase card (acquired under the General Services Administration Smart Pay Program) or the United States of America Card (acquired from the Department of the Treasury).

(5) Acquisition authority as may be appropriate.

b. **Payment Procedures.** Payment shall be made promptly upon the written request (or billing) of the agency or unit filling the order. Payment may be made in advance or upon delivery of the goods or services ordered and shall be for any part of the estimated or actual cost as determined by the activity filling the order. A bill submitted or a request for payment is not subject to audit or certification in advance of payment. Proper adjustment of amounts paid in advance shall be made as agreed to by the heads of the activities on the basis of the actual cost of goods or services provided.

c. **Small Amounts**

(1) Working capital funds, the Corps of Engineers Civil Works Revolving Fund, and other DOD revolving funds may not waive reimbursement of any amount. This does not preclude identification of a central payment office by a DOD component to pay small bills.

(2) When an appropriated fund activity is the performer and the amount to be billed within the same DOD component or to another DOD component is less than $1,000, the billing may be suspended by the billing organization until the end of the fiscal year, or until the total billed exceeds $1,000. However, no later than the end of the fiscal year, all suspended amounts must be billed even though the amount to be billed is less than $1,000.

(3) When the amount to be billed to a non-DOD USG activity is less than $1,000, the billing may be suspended by the billing organization until the end of the fiscal year, or until the total billed exceeds $1,000. However, no later than the end of the fiscal year, all suspended amounts must be billed to non-DOD USG activities even though the amount to be billed is less than $1,000.

6. Reimbursements

a. **Appropriated Funds.** The requesting activity must pay the servicing activity the actual costs of the goods or services provided. Actual costs include all direct costs attributable to providing the goods or services, regardless of whether the servicing activity's expenditures are increased. Actual costs also include indirect costs (overhead) to the extent they have a significant relationship to providing the goods or services and benefit the requesting activity. DOD activities not funded by working capital funds normally do not charge indirect costs to other DOD activities. When contracting out for goods or services, the servicing activity may not require payment of a fee or charge which exceeds the actual cost of entering into and administering the contract (reference FAR 17.505). DODFMR, Volume 11A, *Reimbursable Operations, Policy, and Procedures*, Chapter 1, "General Reimbursement Procedures and Documentation," paragraph 010203, "General Rules for Determining Amounts to be Reimbursed," specifies billing policies and procedures for Economy Act orders. Payment shall be made in accordance with subparagraph 5b, "Ordering Procedures."

b. **Working Capital Fund Activities.** Reimbursable costs in the case of servicing DOD activities operating under a working capital fund shall be determined in accordance with DODFMR, Volume 11B, *Reimbursable Operations, Policy, and Procedures—Working Capital Funds (WCF)*.

7. Accounting

a. Economy Act orders may be issued as direct fund cite orders where the requesting activity identifies the appropriate fund citation for the servicing activity to place on the requested contract or reimbursable orders. Economy Act orders shall neither be administered nor accounted for by servicing DOD activities as separate subdivisions of appropriations or funds similar to an allotment. Appropriation-type accounting for Economy Act orders shall be performed by the requesting DOD component in accordance with the DODFMR, Volume 3, *Budget Execution—Availability and Use of Budgetary Resources*, Chapter 15, "Receipt and Use of Budgetary Resources—Execution Level."

b. The operations of servicing DOD activities financed under a working capital fund shall be accounted for in accordance with Volume 11B, *Reimbursable Operations, Policy, and Procedures—Working Capital Funds (WCF)*, of the DODFMR.

c. Economy Act orders received and accepted are the source of obligational authority in the amount of the order for the performance of the work requested.

d. A cost account, or other device, shall be used to accumulate the costs of performance for all Economy Act orders. Those cost accounts shall serve as a historical basis for determining the amount reimbursable for cost-reimbursement Economy Act orders and as a basis of determining a fixed price for similar future fixed-price Economy Act orders.

e. Billings covering reimbursements shall identify costs by each item listed in the Economy Act order. Such billings shall accommodate the use of a DOD (SmartPay) purchase card or the Department of the Treasury's Intragovernmental Payment and Collection System.

Intentionally Blank

APPENDIX H
JOINT OPERATIONS ENTITLEMENTS AND PAY MATRIX

The following entitlements and pay matrix (see Figure H-1) lists the primary allowances available for military and civilian personnel. This list is not all-inclusive and subject to change. Service components should ensure their members are provided current entitlements and pay information prior to participating in joint operations.

JOINT OPERATIONS ENTITLEMENTS AND PAY MATRIX		
ENTITLEMENT	**REFERENCE**	**REMARKS**
Basic Pay	Title 37, USC, Sections 203, 204, 1009	Varies by grade.
Basic Allowance for Housing (BAH)	Title 37, USC, Sections 403, 405 JFTR, Chapter 10	Reservists are authorized full BAH if called to active duty in support of a contingency. All other deployments, non-contingency, the reserve member must be called to active duty for more than 30 days to be entitled to full BAH. If the deployment is less than 30 days, non-contingency, then the member is only entitled to the BAH-Reserve Component rate.
Basic Allowance for Subsistence (BAS)	Title 37, USC, Section 402 DODFMR 7a, Chapter 25	Enlisted members performing TDY (not associated with permanent change of station travel), temporary field or afloat assignments of 80 days or less, essential unit messing or group travel will retain the BAS entitlement held at their permanent duty station.
Travel Options and/or Per Diem	JFTR Joint Travel Regulations	Combatant commander (CCDR) determinate on of regular TDY, essential unit messing, or field duty. Per diem and incidental expense payment may vary by location.
Hostile Fire Pay	Tile 37, USC, Section 310 DODFMR 7a, Chapter 10 DODI 1340.9	Commander (lowest level of command appropriate) issues statement detailing hostile fire and/or hostile mine explosion incident (identifying each member critical to the hostile fire pay), and sends certification to servicing financial support office, with copy to regional CCDR. Death certificate or injury report suffices if it establishes cause of death or injury was due to hostile fire and/or explosion of hostile mine in a foreign area.
Imminent Danger Pay (IDP) and Danger Pay	Title 37, USC, Section 310 DODFMR 7a, Chapter 10 DODI 1340.9 Title 5, USC, Section 5928 DSSR Chapter 650	Specific geographic area must be designated as IDP area. Effective upon approval by the Office of SecDef. Danger pay provided for civilian employees who accompany US military forces in designated IDP areas.
Hardship Duty Pay -- Location	Title 37, USC, Section 305 DODFMR 7a, Chapter 17 DODI 1340.10 Title II of Overseas Differential and Allowances Act (PL 86-707) DSSR 510	Paid to officer, enlisted, and civilian employees only in designated (foreign duty) areas.
Family Separation Allowance	Title 37, USC, Section 427 DODFMR 7a, Chapter 27	Separation from dependents for more than 30 days.

Special Leave Accrual	Title 10, USC, Section 701, 703 DODI 1327.6	Members can accrue a leave balance of up to 120 days if deployed at least 120 days to IDP area or in direct support of mission as certified by the commander.
Combat Zone Tax Exclusion Qualified Hazardous Duty Area Tax Exclusion	Title 26, USC, Section 112 DODFMR 7a, Chapter 44 PL 104-117, 20 March 96 PL 106-21, 10 April 99 DODFMR 7a, Chapter 44 440102-440103	Full basic pay exempt for enlisted personnel and warrant officers. Commissioned officers exemption is equal to the highest amount applicable for enlisted personnel. Combat zone is designated by executive order. Qualified hazardous duty has been declared for contingency operations in Bosnia and Herzegovina by PL 104-117 and the former Yugoslavia by PL 106-21.
Sea Duty Pay	Title 37, USC, Section 305a	Eligibility varies by grade and sea duty time.
UN Entitlements, Leave, Per Diem, and/or Mission Subsistence Allowance and Station Allowances	SecDef Memorandum, 27 January 94 SecDef Memorandum, 1 December 94 JFTR, Volume 1, paragraph U 4155 and U 9302	US personnel may not accept direct compensation from the UN when serving in peacekeeping operations. Special rules apply to use of UN leave.
Savings Deposit Program	DODFMR, Volume 7A, Chapter 51	Amounts up to $10K can be deposited at the rate of 10% per annum.
Legend		
CCDR	combatant commander	
DODFMR	Department of Defense Financial Management Regulation	
DODI	Department of Defense instruction	
DSSR	Department of State Standardized Regulations	
IDP	Imminent Danger Pay	
JFTR	Joint Federal Travel Regulations	
PL	public law	
SecDef	Secretary of Defense	
TDY	temporary duty	
UN	United Nations	
USC	United States Code	

Figure H-1. Joint Operations Entitlements and Pay Matrix

APPENDIX J
SYSTEM REQUIREMENTS AND INTERFACES FOR SERVICES AND DEFENSE FINANCE AND ACCOUNTING SERVICE ACCOUNTING SYSTEMS

1. Overview

a. DFAS is the principal advisor to SecDef for budgetary and fiscal matters and, as such, is responsible for coordinating and collaborating with all DOD agency directors, the Service Chiefs, and the CCDRs that provide warfighting capabilities for America's defense.

b. This appendix provides an outline of FM systems interfacing with accounting and finance systems operated and maintained by DFAS.

2. Accounting Systems

a. **Financial Management System.** The DOD Financial Management System consists of a triad architecture. The three segments of the triad are as follows: Planning, Programming, and Budgeting and Execution process; Army, Navy, Air Force, and DOD agency accounting systems; and all other systems that provide financial information to management.

b. **The Defense Business Systems Management Committee (DBSMC)** oversees transformation in the business mission area and ensures the needs and priorities of the warfighter are met. The DBSMC sets business transformation priorities and recommends the policies and procedures required to attain cross-DOD, end-to-end interoperability of DOD business systems and processes. Specifically, the DBSMC reviews and approves all major releases of the Business Enterprise Architecture and Enterprise Transition Plan. The DBSMC also approves business systems investment decisions and continually monitors schedule and milestone.

c. The **General Accounting and Finance System (GAFS)** is an installation level accounting system in support of the United States Air Force (USAF).

d. **General Fund Enterprise Business System** is a web-based system that allows the US Army to share financial and accounting data across the Service.

e. The **Standard Accounting, Budget, and Reporting System** provides full accounting support for all US Marine Corps general funds and support of departmental level accounting/reporting processes in compliance with federal FM requirements.

f. The **Standard Operation and Maintenance Army Research and Development System (SOMARDS)** is a comprehensive, computerized accounting system designed to serve as the standard system for US Army logistic organizations. It is a complex combination of database files, applications, interfaces, accounting procedures, and transactions which provides for the input of accounting, labor, general ledger, and other miscellaneous transactions by both online and batch processes and by system interfaces.

SOMARDS Non-Technical (SOMARDS NT) controls funds used for purposes such as procurement and TDY travel. The Electronic Commerce Processing Node provides routing and translation services to SOMARDS NT for travel-related financial transactions.

g. The **Defense Travel System (DTS)** is an efficient, flexible system for electronically creating travel authorizations, vouchers, orders, and pre-audit documents and for completing the post-travel claims processes. DTS provides for paperless electronic routing, review, and approval of travel and associated documentation. DTS also uses DOD Common Access Card and Public Key Infrastructure technologies for very high security. DTS includes line of accounting data to ensure payment from the appropriate sources.

h. The **Standard Finance System** is a fully automated, US Army-wide standard accounting system designed to provide sophisticated and comprehensive accounting support at US Army installations and effective "general ledger control" over all resources.

i. The **Standard Accounting and Reporting System (STARS)—Field Level** is an interactive, batch accounting system which provides for processing and reporting of general fund accounting functions for US Navy and other DOD activities.

j. The **STARS—HQ Command Module** is an interactive, batch accounting system which provides for processing and reporting of general fund accounting functions for US Navy and other DOD activities. It maintains the data structure of the record at the document-status level, including all applicable line-of-accounting-level data, for the life cycle of the travel record.

k. The **Defense Working Capital Accounting System (DWAS)** is a fully integrated working capital fund and general fund FM system supporting accounting functions for the Information Services Activity Group—USAF and US Army, the Document Automation and Production Service, the Defense National Stockpile Center, the Naval Facilities Engineering Service Center, and the Public Works Centers Printing and Publication and Navy base support business areas. DWAS is a migratory system that incorporates functionality for general ledger, funds distribution, fixed assets, cost accounting, accounts payables, accounts receivables, billing, contract sales, inventory, and reports.

l. The **Defense Industrial Financial Management System** supports the core FM requirements for the Department of the Navy, US Marine Corps, and USAF depot maintenance and research and development activities. This system is the financial system of record and the central source of consolidated financial information for these DOD activities. The system provides financial reporting, funds control, general ledger, receipts, payment, and cost management functions that enable the customers to produce auditable financial statements.

m. **Transportation Financial Management System-Military (TFMS-M) Surface Deployment and Distribution Command (SDDC).** SDDC's Cost Accounting System is the portion of TFMS-M that uses Oracle Federal Financials and Projects accounting. TFMS-M project accounting is designed to accurately record, classify, and summarize the costs incurred by the Transportation Working Capital Fund (TWCF) for SDDC operations, and to distribute these costs to the appropriate business area in order to recoup the costs from the benefiting customer. Since the TWCF is a working capital fund, it is necessary to make accurate customer billings to preserve the fund corpus.

n. The **MSC—Foreign Military Sales System** is used by the Services and interagency partners to sell defense systems, services, and training to US allies; ensure the proper performance of the functions relating to budgeting, accounting, funds availability, FM systems, financial policy and performance reporting and analysis under the US Navy and TWCF; obtain and justify military and civilian manpower funding; and keep the Commander, Military Sealift Command, informed regarding these matters.

o. **The Defense Enterprise Accounting and Management System** is a DOD-wide FM solution intended for use by United States Transportation Command, USAF, and DFAS. It will replace several existing systems such as GAFS, TFMS-M, and MSC FMS (for TWCF only).

p. **Navy Enterprise Resource Planning** is an integrated business management system that updates and standardizes Navy business operations, provides financial transparency and total asset visibility across the enterprise, and increases effectiveness and efficiency.

3. Pay Systems

a. The **Defense Civilian Pay System** is the standard DOD civilian pay system. The system maintains pay and leave entitlement records, deductions and withholdings, time and attendance data, and other pertinent employee personnel data.

b. The **Defense Joint Military Pay System** is the joint Service system (excluding the US Marine Corps) for pay and entitlements for the Active and Reserve Components.

4. Entitlement Systems

a. The **Computerized Accounts Payable System for Windows** is a microcomputer-based program designed to automate the many processes associated with vendor pay operations. It calculates entitlements and facilitates compliance with the Prompt Payment Act to reduce interest paid, discounts lost, and personnel overtime costs.

b. The **GAFS—DTS** is used to provide installation level accounting support to the USAF.

c. **OnePay** is an online vendor payment system operating in the STARS database environment and integrated with both the STARS Headquarters Command Module and Field Level accounting systems. The single payment system is operated in a teleprocessing environment, but is designed to accept batch invoice input from both EDI and remote site batching systems. It provides invoice tracking, online inquiry, invoice status, and disbursing/reports. OnePay also provides a report of expenditures to the Department of the Treasury in electronic and hardcopy form.

5. Disbursing Systems

a. The **Centralized Disbursing System** is a consolidated DOD disbursing system that makes payments and accepts collections which are sent to accounting for update.

b. The **Deployable Disbursing System (DDS)** meets the need for a single disbursing system that supports disbursing operations deployed in tactical environments. DDS provides automated accounting and disbursing documentation to mobile and remote military operations within contingency locations requiring foreign currency operations. DDS is a client-server, personal computer-based, stand-alone application that is not network-dependent and utilizes whatever communication means are available in each operational area.

6. Defense Finance and Accounting Service Corporate Database Architecture

The **DFAS Corporate Database** enables DTS to interface with the disbursing and accounting systems.

APPENDIX K
INTEGRATED FINANCIAL OPERATIONS PLANNING CONSIDERATIONS

1. Introduction

This appendix describes planning considerations that JFCs and staff will consider as they conduct sustained IFO. It provides an overview of the key partners and stakeholders who routinely participate in financial operations within an operational area; and describes mechanisms and organizational structures that are allowing units involved in current operations in Iraq and Afghanistan to best employ the economic instrument of national power.

2. General

a. IFO are inherently complex, but they can increase momentum in an operational area. Financial operations can include direct funding using currency, business processes, networks of stocks, and/or specific goods and services of value. Ultimately, IFO seeks to increase the effectiveness of all resources spent in an operational area. Based on recent operations, it is clear that when financial operations are not integrated in an operational area, it can lead to contractor inefficiency, unnecessary and duplicative spending, and even the inadvertent funding of adversaries.

b. Employment of IFO confronts the JFC with the challenge of gaining situational awareness across a myriad of organizations and their activities not under the JFC's command and then leveraging those efforts to achieve joint operation/campaign objectives.

c. Financial operations are assets that use elements of the economic instrument of national power to stabilize an area and promote its political and economic development. They are additional tools available to the JFC to create the desired effects and, ultimately, achieve the commander's objectives.

3. Leveraging Partners and Stakeholders

a. Strategic and operational objectives of DOD organizations may not always coincide with the goals and objectives of non-DOD organizations and may not be transparent to other organizations conducting operations within an operational area. IFO calls for visibility and coordination of the multiple ongoing stability and development efforts in a given operational area and the organizations undertaking them. Visibility refers to situational awareness of ongoing financial operations efforts in the operational area by all parties.

b. Improved awareness begins with recognizing the financial footprint in the operational area. Mere presence and the meeting of military requirements to carry out operations, such as contracting with local businesses to provide support to forward operating bases (FOBs) (e.g., fuel, trash disposal), changes the local political and economic dynamic. IFO injects additional money into an environment that may or may not have the capacity to absorb it. Dollars spent supporting FOBs, especially large FOBs, can alter local economic and political power structures, sometimes more than targeted projects meant to influence the population.

This does not entail subordination of requirements by such considerations; however, the JFC needs to recognize financial operations often begin with the simple arrival of military forces in the operational area.

c. Additionally, visibility includes identifying the organizations expending funds in a given operational area, their objectives, sources of funding, capabilities, and how they conduct operations. Gathering and understanding this information will move the JFC and staffs toward coordination with other organizations in the operational area. Depending on the location, the JFC may find needed information on other organizations from the US embassy, the mission director of USAID in the region (if appointed), UN agencies and other IGOs, the NGOs who receive USG funding, or interagency partners at the provincial reconstruction team (PRT) (or similar) level.

d. Coordination of IFO efforts requires extensive effort, which has two parts: synchronization and deconfliction. Synchronization is the arrangement of military actions in time, space, and purpose to produce maximum relative combat power at a decisive place and time. Specific expertise or capabilities could make those implementing partners the best choice to achieve an IFO-related objective or offset a capabilities gap. Deconfliction is avoiding duplication of effort by USG and international contributors, as well as preventing the USG and international stakeholders from working at cross purposes in the operational area. By synchronizing military efforts with other partners, a set of mutual objectives can be recognized, to motivate meaningful coordination. Achieving coordination at any level for financial operations requires an understanding of the types of activities that should be coordinated and the mechanisms and applicable guidance already in existence.

e. Because the solution to a problem when conducting military operations seldom, if ever, resides within the capability of just one organization, joint operation/campaign plans should be crafted to recognize the core competencies of various agencies, and military activities should be coordinated and resources integrated with those of others to achieve the operational objectives. Recent operations in both Iraq and Afghanistan have clearly shown there will not be a single authority over civilian USG agencies with clearly defined roles and responsibilities (i.e., unity of command). At best, "unity of effort" may be achieved. Coordinating and integrating efforts between the joint force and USG agencies, multinational partners, IGOs, and NGOs (which include the for-profit private sector), cannot and should not be equated to the C2 of a military operation. Nonmilitary stakeholders do not have similarly sized resources nor the same mission and reporting requirements. More critically, their perspectives on a situation and possible solutions are different, and the different professional cultures can sometimes clash.

f. These differences present significant coordination challenges. However, the commander should be aware and recognize that these other agencies often possess far greater expertise, and in some cases, more capabilities than the military to execute political, diplomatic, and economic missions. JP 3-08, *Interorganizational Coordination During Joint Operations,* states "the degree to which military and civilian components can be integrated and harmonized will bear directly on efficiency and success." Hence, it is imperative for financial operations that partners in the operational area to be included, whenever possible, in the planning process.

g. A mutual understanding of organizational goals, processes, and procedures is critical for successful IFO. Integration among all the organizations involved in financial operations will improve coordination that should result in greater synchronization and prioritization. This two-way street will allow civilian partners such as the DOS and USAID to provide input into proposed military projects. Some organizations working in the operational area may have separate reporting chains and cannot or will not directly support the JFC in the planning and execution of the joint operation/campaign plan. However, if the methodology suggested within this appendix is implemented, the majority of the stabilization and development efforts in the operational area will be integrated and, consequently, more effective.

h. In most permissive environments, such as Combined Joint Task Force—Horn of Africa, DOD elements are the supporting organization and USG, international, and other organizations will be the supported element. This does not reduce the need to incorporate financial operations into all joint operation/campaign plans to fully leverage all the instruments of national power. The objectives of all USG organizations, including the military, should be nested within the strategic goals of the United States.

> **Currently, Afghanistan is the operational area where the US is decisively engaged in stability operations, and potentially the most complex; therefore, it will be used throughout this appendix as a model. It is recognized that there will be differences in other operational areas. However, the principles contained in this appendix should have global application.**

4. Financial Operations Stakeholders

Several key USG organizations (e.g., DOS and USAID) plan and execute financial operations. The JFC must have situational awareness of their activities and the ability to coordinate with these organizations. Each can play a key role in the civilian-military structure because each has its own substantial funding streams that are independent of joint force funding. However, they have different and distinct missions to accomplish in the operational area. These organizations may have expertise and capabilities not inherent in DOD, which could help achieve the operational objectives if leveraged properly. The organizations include:

a. **US Department of State.** DOS works to advance the freedoms of the international community by helping to build and sustain a more democratic, secure, and prosperous world composed of well-governed states that respond to the needs of their people, reduce widespread poverty, and act responsibly within the international system. DOS performs diplomatic and political reporting and is responsible for the conduct of bilateral relationships with foreign countries and multinational organizations such as the UN. It has direct access to nearly all foreign governments through US embassies. Representatives from nearly every USG organization are attached to the embassy and comprise the country team, under the leadership of the ambassador, to meet, to share information, formally and informally, and to coordinate their efforts within a host country. The ambassador, or chief-of-mission, is the senior US representative and personal envoy of the president in a host country regardless of which agency may have the lead on specific operations. Many organizations within DOS participate in financial operations, either directly managing funds appropriated by Congress or overseeing the policies related to use of those funds. The department's Office of the Coordinator for Reconstruction and Stabilization (S/CRS) is responsible for counterinsurgency (COIN) and crisis stabilization matters. The mission of S/CRS is to lead, coordinate, and institutionalize USG civilian capacity to prevent or prepare for post-conflict situations, and to help stabilize and reconstruct societies in transition from conflict or civil strife, so they can reach a sustainable path toward peace, democracy, and a market economy. S/CRS is an interagency team staffed by various USG representatives to lead the civilian component, in concert with military forces, in the coordination of stabilization and reconstruction efforts. It includes members from DOS, USAID, Office of the Secretary of Defense, CIA, Army Corps of Engineers, Joint Chiefs of Staff, and the Department of the Treasury. In the Afghanistan operational area any high-level contact or policy action necessary (with either the Afghanistan or the Pakistani governments) are generally executed via DOS and the ambassador's country team.

b. **US Agency for International Development.** USAID is a semi-independent agency that provides economic, development, and humanitarian assistance around the world in support of the foreign policy goals of the United States. USAID receives policy guidance and increasingly programmatic direction from DOS. The USAID Administrator leads the agency in Washington, DC, and serves as a Deputy Secretary equivalent. The USAID Administrator's in-country representative is the mission director. Sometimes located at the US embassy, or in their own building, the mission director is the one in charge of all USAID activities in each country. DOS does provide foreign policy guidance. USAID is organized into geographic and functional bureaus as well as independent offices. Geographic bureaus manage overall activities within the countries USAID has programs, whereas functional bureaus manage programs that are worldwide or cross borders. USAID is focused on three primary program areas: economic growth, agriculture, and trade; global health; and democracy, conflict prevention, and humanitarian assistance and is the implementing body of most US foreign assistance funds around the globe.

(1) Many USAID personnel are trained and experienced in the conduct of development operations in post-conflict environments. In addition to US foreign service and civil service officers, USAID employs a large number of foreign nationals at overseas missions to help administer its assistance programs. Most programs are implemented through for profit contractors and not-for-profit grantees. These NGOs are the means through which USAID implements its operations. When operating in a country, military personnel are likely to meet USAID representatives in the capital cities and in PRTs.

(2) USAID operates on a different planning horizon than DOD. As with all development efforts, USAID operates in a supporting role to foreign governments and communities, as dictated by the pace set by the local population, where progress may be measured in terms of decades or generations rather than year-to-year. When operating closely with military forces, it is important that USAID's effectiveness, and that of its

implementing partners, not be diminished by local perceptions that they are engaged in military or intelligence operations. Depending on the operational situation, coordination with USAID, its partners, and other development organizations, should be accomplished in a manner consistent with USAID policies and goals.

(3) USAID receives all of its funding under the FAA of 1961, which is congressionally approved each year. USAID is one of a very few federal departments and agencies that can receive funds directly from private sources (e.g., corporations and charities) to be used in partnerships.

c. **Additional US Government Departments and Agencies.** Other USG departments and agencies participating in the execution of financial operations include the Department of Agriculture, Department of Health and Human Services, and Department of Education. Agencies supporting counter threat finance (CTF) efforts include the Department of Justice, Department of the Treasury, Drug Enforcement Administration, and the CIA.

d. **PRT.** The focus of the PRT is on the provincial government and local infrastructure in the area assigned. The organization and size of the PRT will vary largely depending on the operational environment and required tasks. The PRT leader is normally a DOS official but may in some cases be a DOD official.

(1) PRTs manage teams of international civil-military affairs specialists and often have excellent knowledge of and relationships with local Afghans and local Afghan government officials in their areas of operation. Those PRTs' mission is to support the growth and increased capacity of the HN through securing areas so that reconstruction efforts can proceed, as well as providing support for humanitarian assistance. Teams can be from a single nation or multinational. They can consist of about eighty people – sixty who are experts in foreign affairs, agriculture, and engineering while the remaining twenty are civilian specialists who work with Afghan partners.

(2) Funding is perhaps the most difficult issue for PRT management. Funding will come from several different sources, even within a single executive department. Projects conducted by US led PRTs may use the CERP monies or such other funds as Congress may authorize. CERP requests for large projects must receive the approval of the higher HQ. Non-US led PRTs do have access to CERP; a majority of the funding comes from their respective nations. For nations that do not provide funds to their PRTs, the funds are received from the UN or the HN. Funds also come from the USAID representative (local governance and community development program) embedded with the PRT. The USAID representative does not have the authority to dispense funds for high cost projects; that must come from certified contracting officers. The local governance and community development fund is the only USAID monies available to the PRTs. At the operational level, the PRTs are vital hubs where civil-military efforts are concentrated before they reach out like spokes to the surrounding local population.

INTERAGENCY COORDINATION

An example of a provincial reconstruction team (PRT) and military coordination was within the US Forces-Iraq operational area, where each PRT had a work plan synchronized with the military's operations plan. The PRTs in Iraq were all coordinated through the US Embassy's Office of Provincial Affairs (OPA). US forces lent military officers to the OPA to assist in the planning and coordination of activities. The officers were integrated with the OPA staff and actually reported to the Director of the OPA.

e. **Nongovernmental Organizations.** Other stakeholders, such as NGOs and the private sector, directly affect the conduct of operations, including financial operations. Therefore, the JFC requires situational awareness of their activities so that they can be accounted for in joint operation/campaign planning.

5. **Coordinating Counter Threat Finance**

a. In accordance with Title 10, USC, Section 113, DODD 5205.14, *DOD Counter Threat Finance (CTF) Policy*, establishes DOD policy and assigns DOD responsibilities for the conduct of CTF. CTF is the means to detect, counter, contain, disrupt, deter, or dismantle the transnational financing of state and non-state adversaries threatening US national security. Monitoring, assessing, analyzing, and exploiting financial information are key support functions for CTF activities. CTF is not operational area specific: because it looks at the flow of money across several operational areas, it is a global effort, not just a regional one. CTF activities include, but are not limited to, countering narcotics trafficking, proliferation activities, weapons of mass destruction networks, trafficking in persons, weapons trafficking, precursor chemical smuggling, terrorist revenue and logistics, anti-corruption, and other such activities that generate revenue through illicit networks. It is critical for those conducting CTF to maintain a strong link with financial execution elements. For example, in Afghanistan, insurgent and criminal elements have been receiving funds from coalition or even USG sources because those executing funds in the operational area did not know which contractors or companies had criminal or insurgent ties. CTF operators have that information and need to get it to those executing IFO before contracts are approved and funded.

b. CTF can allow the JFC to deny adversaries access to vital funding streams by identifying the sources and conduits of funding along with which insurgent elements utilize them. If integrated into the overall visibility of IFO, it provides the JFC more data directed to enemy activities, and action can be taken to deny the enemy not only access to funding, but deny the enemy the ability to conduct operations in the operational area. CTF can provide valuable intelligence to operators if intelligence collectors are aware of CTF sufficiently enough to recognize the usefulness of financial intelligence. This includes financial document exploitation and providing appropriate instructions for authorized collectors of intelligence on how to obtain CTF-related information. Such information could help prevent US funds from inadvertently flowing to the insurgencies and allow operators to target or capture insurgents involved in illicit financial activities.

c. CTF can contribute to COIN by eliminating insurgent funding and identifying host government corruption. A legitimate host government is vital to successful COIN. While protection of sources and methods is always an important consideration, a host government often cannot effectively deal with corruption because it lacks hard data on which to build cases against corrupt officials. The dilemma for the JFC in sharing corruption-fighting information with a host government is that it can allow corrupt officials to discover potential action being taken against them. Not sharing information on corrupt officials likely will allow them to continue their illicit activities. Further, targeting or arrests by non-HN authorities can further erode the host government's legitimacy in the eyes of the population.

d. Effective IFO requires sharing of data between those entities specializing in CTF and financial executors. Examples of data sharing that CTF entities could provide are information on possible front companies and individuals and financial organizations with both legitimate and illegitimate business interests to ensure coalition funds are not unwittingly being used to finance the insurgency. Those who are executing funds, such as contracting commands and USAID, collect information, including vendor databases, audit information on specific companies and vendor employee lists which would likely be of value to the CTF stakeholders in their efforts to disrupt the enemy's financial networks. This type of information could also enhance CTF anticorruption efforts.

e. CTF is a consideration in all steps of the IFO process and should be a primary concern in evaluation of projects, selection of conduits or implementers, and assessment. The information derived in this process from a variety of sources can contribute to the knowledge base required for effective CTF.

6. Operational Coordinating Mechanism

a. **Key Implications.** The perceived advantages of participation in an IFO cross-functional collaboration by member organizations are an important factor in maximizing cooperation and mutual benefit. Partners will participate only if there is benefit to their own objectives. Development of a "win-win" situation will produce advantages in increased information sharing and cooperation. The JFC, when organizing to conduct IFO, must consider several key implications.

(1) **There is no "one-size-fits-all" membership in the IFO organization.** The structural arrangement must account for different levels of involvement when designing the guidelines for the organization responsible for financial operations. The time horizon of projects and individual organizational objectives may require participants to move in and out of the agreed upon structure depending on the level of activity/interest.

(2) **Terms of reference need to be in place early in the process.** Roles, responsibilities, and expectations need to be defined upfront to avoid participants coming to the table with unrealistic expectations. The terms of reference must create a mutually beneficial situation for all participants, or membership will quickly diminish if they do not see the value of their organization's participation.

(3) **Different structures and leadership relationships should be considered, depending on the operational environment.** The JFC should consider different management/leadership structures (e.g., civilian, military, or co-lead) in order to improve the effectiveness of this body responsible for financial operations in the JTF. Personality of the lead is extremely important, and he/she must contend with organizational and cultural differences.

b. Regardless the structure, interrelationships will exist between key financial operators which must be managed by the JFC (Figure K-1).

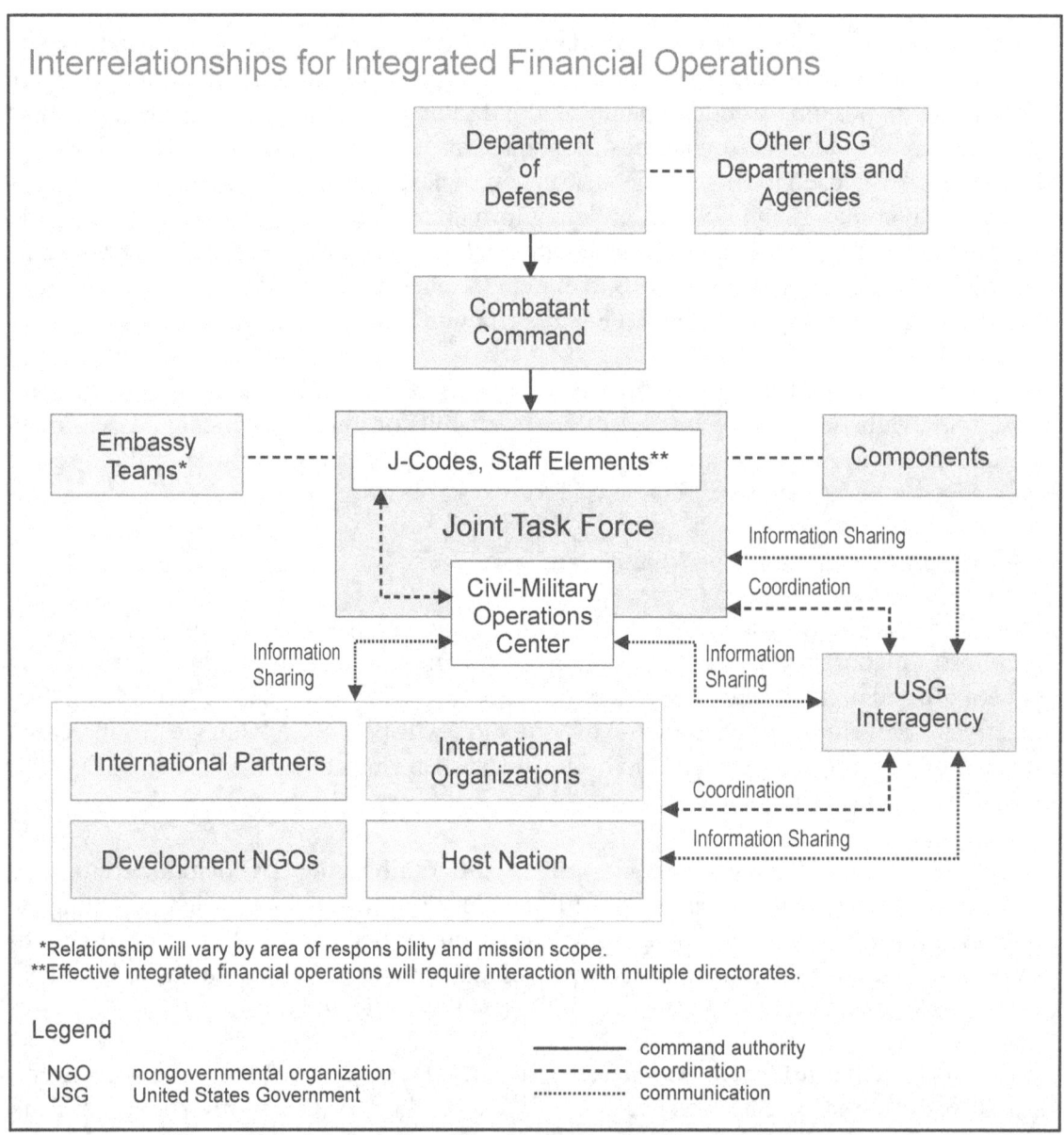

Figure K-1. Interrelationships for Integrated Financial Operations

c. **Adapting the Civil-Military Operations Center (CMOC).** Joint planning integrates military actions with those of other instruments of national power and our multinational partners in time, space, and purpose to achieve a specified end state. Since IFO will integrate the efforts of disparate organizations, a means of applying the elements of the IFO process in this complex environment is required. Therefore, structures and processes that reflect this condition emerge as most appropriate to the planning, execution, and assessment of IFO. A structure described in JP 3-08, *Interorganizational Coordination During Joint Operations,* the CMOC, provides a means of overcoming the significant challenges of operating with multiple organizational cultures, histories, and objectives; and incorporating IFO into the joint planning process. Although doctrinally the CMOC is not restricted to any specific operational level, most of its previous employments have been primarily at the tactical level. Therefore, its perception as a tactical level construct must be considered. The JFC could elect to utilize a joint interagency coordination group or other cross-functional staffing arrangement for the conduct of IFO. The more important factors are the roles, responsibilities, and functions of the organization for planning, execution, and assessment of IFO, not its name. The discussions that follow will use "CMOC" as a title, with the understanding that the name of the construct is not fixed or mandated.

(1) The CMOC is a mechanism that can serve as the primary coordination interface for operational and tactical level coordination between the JFC and other stakeholders. A CMOC may include representatives of US military forces, other USG agencies, multinational partners, IGOs, NGOs, and the private sector.

(2) Conducting the interagency coordination required for IFO requires a departure from traditional military thinking. The legacy requirement for C2 is not appropriate for operational structures and environments where the military commander does not possess clear authority over all activities in the assigned operational area. As a result, coordination and collaboration are more applicable to gaining unity of effort. As with all interagency activities, effective IFO will require inclusion, vice exclusion, of external stakeholders that mandates an understanding of the different roles, authorities, missions, culture, and processes of external stakeholders. Due to the inclusive nature of IFO, a rigid hierarchical structure is not appropriate. One of the benefits of the CMOC-like structure is that it is exceptionally flexible and designed to conform to the needs of the JTF. Hence, the specific composition of the CMOC will be based on the requirements of the individual JFC. Importantly, the JFC's level of the authority is limited.

(3) While the JFC can exercise command authority over assigned and attached forces participating organizations outside DOD will not reflect "unity of command" with one single authority and clearly defined roles and responsibilities. At various times, the JFC draws on the capabilities of other USG agencies, provides capabilities to other organizations, or merely deconflicts joint force activities with those of others. The JFC may have some form of supported or supporting relationships with IGOs; however, in some operations, USG agencies' relationships with IGOs are voluntary and based upon shared goals and good will. The relationship between the JFC and the leadership of NGOs is neither supported nor supporting. These conditions make the roles and responsibilities for IFO complex and

demanding. Accordingly, the CMOC likely will exercise C2, coordination, or simply information sharing concurrently with the various organizations engaged in IFO.

(4) The capabilities required for IFO are independent of the specific structure employed. With the CMOC approach, there is not a "one size fits all" structure appropriate to all areas of operations, scenarios, and missions. The organizational structure and composition is less important than the possession of the capabilities to perform the functions described in the following subsection.

(5) Doctrinally, the CMOC structure is fluid and adaptable to the local conditions and command mission. The CMOC role extends beyond purely financial operations. The JFC already may have a functioning CMOC for conduct of CMO. In those cases, where the roles and responsibilities for the CMOC are established, modification of the existing structure is preferred over creation of a new configuration. However, independent of the membership and organization selected, the CMOC would perform specific IFO tasks.

d. Conducting the interagency coordination required for IFO requires a departure from traditional military thinking. The legacy requirement for C2 is not appropriate for operational structures and environments where the military commander does not possess clear authority over all activities in the assigned operational area. As a result, coordination and collaboration are more applicable to gaining unity of effort. As with all interagency activities, effective IFO will require inclusion, vice exclusion, of external stakeholders that mandates an understanding of the different roles, authorities, missions, culture, and processes of external stakeholders. Due to the inclusive nature of IFO, a rigid hierarchical structure is not appropriate. One of the benefits of the CMOC-like structure is that it is exceptionally flexible and designed to conform to the needs of the JTF. Hence, the specific composition of a CMOC would be based on the requirements of the individual JFC. Importantly, the level of the authority of the JFC is limited.

e. While the JFC can exercise command authority over assigned and attached forces outside DOD, participating organizations will not reflect "unity of command" with one single authority and clearly defined roles and responsibilities. At various times, the JFC draws on the capabilities of other USG agencies, provides capabilities to other organizations, or merely deconflicts joint force activities with those of others. The JFC may have some form of supported or supporting relationships with IGOs; however, in some operations, USG agencies' relationships with IGOs are voluntary and based upon shared goals and good will. The relationship between the JFC and the leadership of NGOs is neither supported nor supporting. These conditions make the roles and responsibilities for IFO complex and demanding.

APPENDIX L
REFERENCES

The development of JP 1-06, *Financial Management Support in Joint Operations,* is based upon the following primary references:

1. General

    a. Title 6, USC.

    b. Title 10, USC.

    c. Title 14, USC.

    d. Title 22, USC.

    e. Title 31, USC.

    f. Title 32, USC.

    g. Title 37, USC.

    h. Title 41, USC.

    i. Chief Financial Officers Act of 1990.

    j. Federal Financial Management Improvement Act of 1996.

    k. Government Management and Reform Act of 1994.

    l. OMB Circular A-11, *Preparation, Submission, and Execution of the Budget.*

    m. OMB Circular A-123, *Management's Responsibility for Internal Control.*

    n. Joint Federal Travel Regulation and Joint Travel Regulation.

    o. Joint Plan for DOD Noncombatant Evacuation and Repatriation.

    p. Public Law 100-461, Foreign Operations, Export Financing, and Related Programs Appropriation Act.

    q. Public Law 101-165, Title V, Emergency Response Fund.

    r. Public Law 103-139, Sec 8131, Emergency Response.

2. Department of Defense Publications

a. DODD 1404.10, *DOD Civilian Expeditionary Workforce.*

b. DODD 5100.1, *Functions of the Department of Defense and Its Major Components.*

c. DODD 5100.3, *Support of the Headquarters of Combatant and Subordinate Joint Commands.*

d. DODD 5205.14, *DOD Counter Threat Finance (CTF) Policy.*

e. DODI 4000.19, *Interservice and Intragovernmental Support.*

f. DODI 5010.40, *Manager's Internal Control Program (MICP) Procedures.*

g. DODI 7000.14, *Department of Defense Financial Management Policy and Procedures.*

h. DOD 7000.14-R, *Department of Defense Financial Management Regulations (FMRs).*

i. DOD 5105.38M, *Security Assistance Management Manual.*

j. DSCA Handbook, *Foreign Assistance Act (FAA) Drawdown of Defense Articles and Services.*

3. Chairman of the Joint Chiefs of Staff Publications

a. JP 1-0, *Joint Personnel Support.*

b. JP 1-02, *Department of Defense Dictionary of Military and Associated Terms.*

c. JP 3-0, *Joint Operations.*

d. JP 3-07.3, *Peace Operations.*

e. JP 3-08, *Interorganizational Coordination During Joint Operations.*

f. JP 3-16, *Multinational Operations.*

g. JP 3-28, *Defense Support of Civil Authorities.*

h. JP 3-33, *Joint Task Force Headquarters.*

i. JP 3-57, *Civil-Military Operation.*

j. JP 3-68, *Noncombatant Evacuation Operations*.

k. JP 4-10, *Operational Contract Support*.

l. JP 5-0, *Joint Operation Planning*.

m. CJCSI 2120.01B, *Acquisition and Cross-Servicing Agreements*.

n. CJCSI 3290.01C, *Program for Detainee Operations*.

o. CJCSI 5120.02B, *Joint Doctrine Development System*.

p. CJCSI 7201.01B, *Combatant Commander's Official Representation Funds (ORF)*.

q. CJCSI 7401.01E, *Combatant Commander Initiative Fund (CCIF)*.

r. CJCSM 3122.03C, *Joint Operation Planning and Execution System (JOPES), Volume 2, Planning Formats*.

4. **Service Publications**

a. Field Manual 1-06, *Financial Management Operations*.

b. Army Regulation 27-20, *Claims*.

c. Army Regulation 190-8, *Enemy Prisoners of War-Administration, Employment and Compensation*.

d. Army Regulation 190-57, *Civilian Internees-Administration, Employment and Compensation*.

e. Air Force Handbook 65-115, *Guide to FM Expeditionary Deployments*.

f. Air Force Instruction 10-213, *Comptroller Operations Under Emergency Conditions*.

g. Air Force Policy Directive 65-1, *Management of Financial Services*.

h. Air Force Instruction 65-601, Volume 1, *USAF Budget Guidance and Procedures*.

i. Air Force Pamphlet 65-110, *Deployed Agent Operations*.

j. Department of the Navy Manual NAVSO P-1000, *Financial Management Policy Manual*.

5. Multinational Publications

NATO STANAG 6007, *Financial Principles and Procedures for the Provision of Support Within NATO.*

APPENDIX M
ADMINISTRATIVE INSTRUCTIONS

1. User Comments

Users in the field are highly encouraged to submit comments on this publication to: Deputy Director, J-7 Joint Staff, Joint and Coalition Warfighting, ATTN: Joint Doctrine Support Division, 116 Lake View Parkway, Suffolk, VA 23435-2697. These comments should address content (accuracy, usefulness, consistency, and organization), writing, and appearance.

2. Authorship

The lead agent for this publication is the Director for Operational Plans and Joint Force Development J-7. The Joint Staff doctrine sponsor for this publication is the Director for Force Structure, Resource, and Assessment, Joint Staff J-8.

3. Supersession

This publication supersedes JP 1-06, 4 March 2008, *Financial Management Support in Joint Operations*.

4. Change Recommendations

a. Recommendations for urgent changes to this publication should be submitted:

TO: JOINT STAFF SUFFOLK VA//JCW-JDSD//
INFO: JOINT STAFF WASHINGTON DC//J7-JEDD/J-8//

b. Routine changes should be submitted electronically to the Deputy Director, J-7 Joint Staff, Joint and Coalition Warfighting, Joint Doctrine Support Division and info the Lead Agent and the Director for Operational Plans and Joint Force Development J-7/JEDD via the CJCS JEL at http://www.dtic.mil/doctrine.

c. When a Joint Staff directorate submits a proposal to the CJCS that would change source document information reflected in this publication, that directorate will include a proposed change to this publication as an enclosure to its proposal. The Military Services and other organizations are requested to notify the Joint Staff J-7 when changes to source documents reflected in this publication are initiated.

5. Distribution of Publications

Local reproduction is authorized and access to unclassified publications is unrestricted. However, access to and reproduction authorization for classified JPs must be in accordance with DOD Regulation 5200.1-R, *Information Security Program*.

6. Distribution of Electronic Publications

a. Joint Staff J-7 will not print copies of JPs for distribution. Electronic versions are available on JDEIS at https://jdeis.js.mil (NIPRNET), and https://jdeis.js.smil.mil (SIPRNET) and on the JEL at http://www.dtic.mil/doctrine (NIPRNET).

b. Only approved JPs and joint test publications are releasable outside the combatant commands, Services, and Joint Staff. Release of any classified JP to foreign governments or foreign nationals must be requested through the local embassy (Defense Attaché Office) to DIA, Defense Foreign Liaison/IE-3, 200 MacDill Blvd., Joint Base Anacostia-Bolling, Washington, DC 20340-5100.

c. JEL CD-ROM. Upon request of a joint doctrine development community member, the Joint Staff J-7 will produce and deliver one CD-ROM with current JPs. This JEL CD-ROM will be updated not less than semi-annually and when received can be locally reproduced for use within the combatant commands and Services.

GLOSSARY
PART I—ABBREVIATIONS AND ACRONYMS

ACSA	acquisition and cross-servicing agreement
AECA	Arms Export Control Act
AIK	assistance in kind
AOR	area of responsibility
ASD(SO/LIC)	Assistant Secretary of Defense (Special Operations and Low-Intensity Conflict)
C2	command and control
CCDR	combatant commander
CCIF	Combatant Commander Initiative Fund
CERP	Commanders' Emergency Response Program
CI	civilian internee
CIA	Central Intelligence Agency
CJCS	Chairman of the Joint Chiefs of Staff
CJCSI	Chairman of the Joint Chiefs of Staff instruction
CJCSM	Chairman of the Joint Chiefs of Staff manual
CMO	civil-military operations
CMOC	civil-military operations center
COA	course of action
COIN	counterinsurgency
CRA	continuing resolution authority
CTF	counter threat finance
CUL	common-user logistics
CVS	commercial vendor services
D&F	determinations and findings
DBSMC	Defense Business Systems Management Committee
DD	Department of Defense (form)
DDS	Deployable Disbursing System
DFAS	Defense Finance and Accounting Service
DHP	Defense Health Program
DOD	Department of Defense
DODD	Department of Defense directive
DODFMR	Department of Defense Financial Management Regulation
DOS	Department of State
DSCA	Defense Security Cooperation Agency
DSSR	Department of State Standardized Regulation
DTS	Defense Travel System
DWAS	Defense Working Capital Accounting System
EA	executive agent
EDI	electronic data interchange

EEE	emergency and extraordinary expense
EFT	electronic funds transfer
EPW	enemy prisoner of war
ESF	Economic Support Fund
EVE	equal value exchange
FAA	Foreign Assistance Act
FAR	Federal Acquisition Regulation
FCA	Foreign Claims Act
FHA	foreign humanitarian assistance
FM	financial management
FMS	foreign military sales
FNS	foreign nation support
FOB	forward operating base
GAFS	General Accounting and Finance System
GAO	Government Accountability Office
GCC	geographic combatant commander
HCA	humanitarian and civic assistance
HN	host nation
HNS	host-nation support
HQ	headquarters
IFO	integrated financial operations
IGO	intergovernmental organization
IMET	international military education and training
J-1	manpower and personnel directorate of a joint staff
J-2	intelligence directorate of a joint staff
J-4	logistics directorate of a joint staff
J-5	plans directorate of a joint staff
J-8	Joint Staff Directorate for Force Structure, Resource, and Assessment
JARB	joint acquisition review board
JFC	joint force commander
JFTR	joint Federal travel regulations
JFUB	joint facilities utilization board
JOA	joint operations area
JOPES	Joint Operation Planning and Execution System
JP	joint publication
JRCC	joint reception coordination center
JTF	joint task force
JTR	joint travel regulations
LDA	limited depository account
LOA	letter of assist

M	million
MILCON	military construction
MIPR	military interdepartmental purchase request
MOA	memorandum of agreement
MSC	Military Sealift Command
MWR	morale, welfare, and recreation
NATO	North Atlantic Treaty Organization
NEO	noncombatant evacuation operation
NGO	nongovernmental organization
O&M	operation and maintenance
OMB	Office of Management and Budget
OPLAN	operation plan
OPORD	operation order
OPTEMPO	operating tempo
OUSD(C/CFO)	Office of the Under Secretary of Defense (Comptroller/Chief Financial Officer)
PIC	payment in cash
PKO	peacekeeping operations
POL	petroleum, oils, and lubricants
PRT	provincial reconstruction team
RBA	reimbursable budget authority
RIK	replacement in kind
RM	resource management
S/CRS	Office of the Coordinator for Reconstruction and Stabilization (DOS)
SDDC	Surface Deployment and Distribution Command
SecDef	Secretary of Defense
SF	standard form
SJA	staff judge advocate
SOMARDS	Standard Operation and Maintenance Army Research and Development System
SOMARDS NT	Standard Operation and Maintenance Army Research and Development System Non-Technical
STANAG	standardization agreement (NATO)
STARS	Standard Accounting and Reporting System
SVC	stored value card
TCA	traditional combatant commander activity
TDY	temporary duty

TFMS-M	Transportation Financial Management System-Military
TWCF	Transportation Working Capital Fund
UN	United Nations
UNPA	United Nations Participation Act
USAF	United States Air Force
USAID	United States Agency for International Development
USC	United States Code
USD(C/CFO)	Under Secretary of Defense (Comptroller/Chief Financial Officer)
USD(P)	Under Secretary of Defense for Policy
USG	United States Government
USNORTHCOM	United States Northern Command
USSOCOM	United States Special Operations Command
USUN	United States Mission to the United Nations

PART II—TERMS AND DEFINITIONS

antideficiency violations. The incurring of obligations or the making of expenditure (outlays) in violation of appropriation law as to purpose, time, and amounts as specified in the defense appropriation or appropriations of funds. (JP 1-02. SOURCE: JP 1-06)

assistance in kind. The provision of material and services for a logistic exchange of materials and services of equal value between the governments of eligible countries. Also called **AIK.** (JP 1-02. SOURCE: JP 1-06)

baseline costs. The continuing annual costs of military operations funded by the operations and maintenance and military personnel appropriations. (JP 1-02. SOURCE: JP 1-06)

finance support. A financial management function to provide financial advice and recommendations, pay support, disbursing support, establishment of local depository accounts, essential accounting support, and support of the procurement process. (JP 1-02. SOURCE: JP 1-06)

financial management. The combination of the two core functions of resource management and finance support. Also called **FM.** (Approved for incorporation into JP 1-02.)

foreign nation support. Civil and/or military assistance rendered to a nation when operating outside its national boundaries during military operations based on agreements mutually concluded between nations or on behalf of intergovernmental organizations. Also called **FNS.** (Approved for incorporation into JP 1-02.)

incremental costs. Costs which are additional costs to the Service appropriations that would not have been incurred absent support of the contingency operation. (JP 1-02. SOURCE: JP 1-06)

integrated financial operations. The integration, synchronization, prioritization, and targeting of fiscal resources and capabilities across United States departments and agencies, multinational partners, and nongovernmental organizations against an adversary and in support of the population. Also called **IFO.** (Approved for inclusion in JP 1-02.)

letter of assist. A contractual document issued by the United Nations to a government authorizing it to provide goods or services to a peacekeeping operation. Also called **LOA.** (Approved for incorporation into JP 1-02.)

offset costs. Costs for which funds have been appropriated that may not be incurred as a result of a contingency operation. (Approved for incorporation into JP1-02.)

resource management. A financial management function that provides advice and guidance to the commander to develop command resource requirements. Also called **RM.** (Approved for incorporation into JP 1-02.)

revolving fund account. An account authorized by specific provisions of law to finance a continuing cycle of business-type operations, and which are authorized to incur obligations and expenditures that generate receipts. (Approved for replacement of "revolving fund" and its definition in JP 1-02.)

solatium. Monetary compensation given in areas where it is culturally appropriate to alleviate grief, suffering, and anxiety resulting from injuries, death, and property loss with a monetary payment. (JP 1-02. SOURCE: JP 1-06.)

training aid. Any item developed or procured with the primary intent that it shall assist in training and the process of learning. (Approved for replacement of "training aids" in JP 1-02.)

working capital fund. A revolving fund established to finance inventories of supplies and other stores, or to provide working capital for industrial-type activities. (JP 1-02. SOURCE: JP 1-06)

JOINT DOCTRINE PUBLICATIONS HIERARCHY

JP 1
JOINT DOCTRINE
JP 1-0
PERSONNEL
JP 2-0
INTELLIGENCE
JP 3-0
OPERATIONS
JP 4-0
LOGISTICS
JP 5-0
PLANS
JP 6-0
COMMUNICATIONS SYSTEM

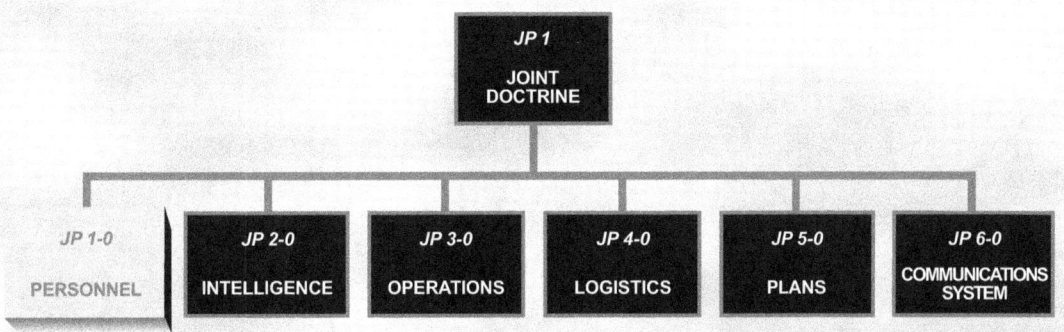

All joint publications are organized into a comprehensive hierarchy as shown in the chart above. **Joint Publication (JP) 1-06** is in the **Personnel** series of joint doctrine publications. The diagram below illustrates an overview of the development process:

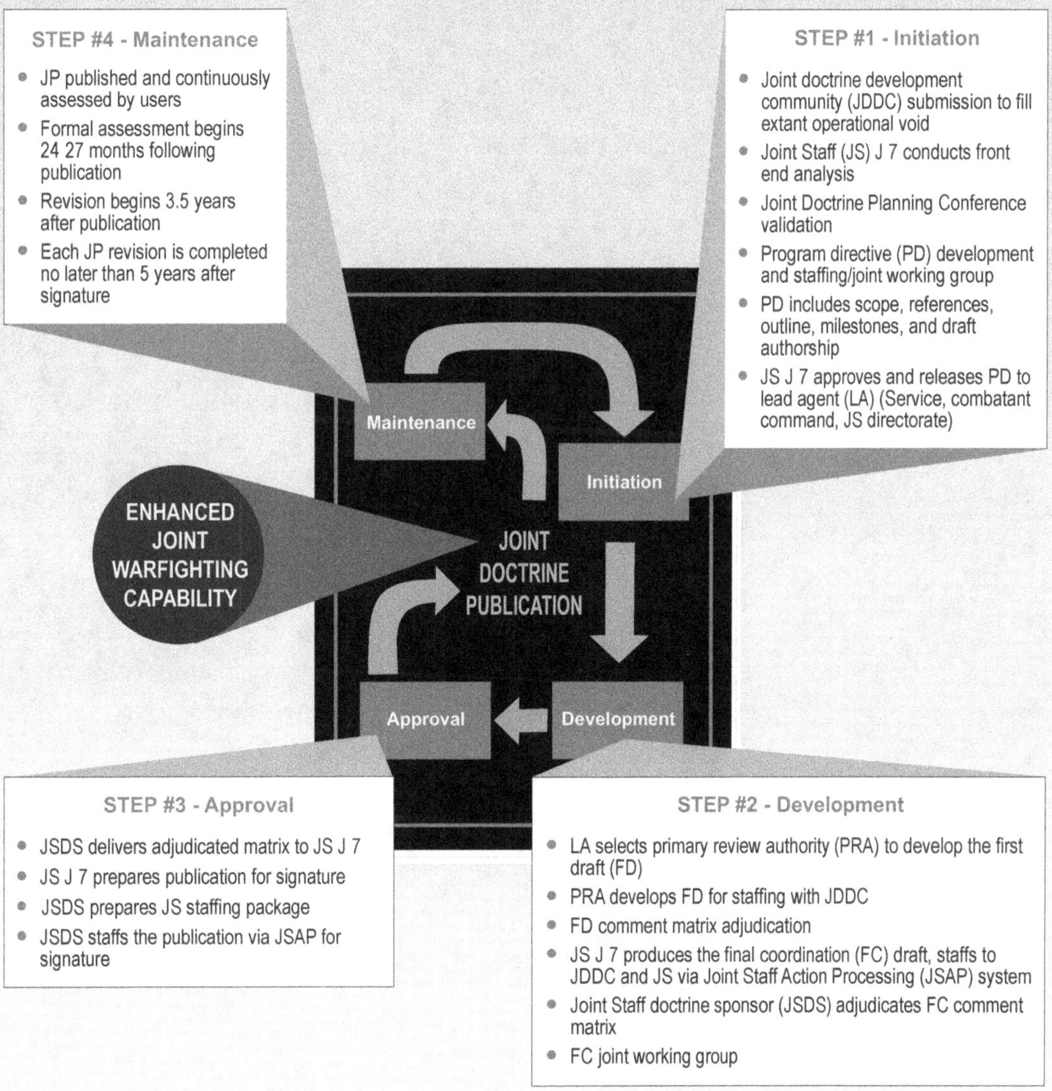

STEP #4 - Maintenance
• JP published and continuously assessed by users
• Formal assessment begins 24 27 months following publication
• Revision begins 3.5 years after publication
• Each JP revision is completed no later than 5 years after signature
STEP #1 - Initiation
• Joint doctrine development community (JDDC) submission to fill extant operational void
• Joint Staff (JS) J 7 conducts front end analysis
• Joint Doctrine Planning Conference validation
• Program directive (PD) development and staffing/joint working group
• PD includes scope, references, outline, milestones, and draft authorship
• JS J 7 approves and releases PD to lead agent (LA) (Service, combatant command, JS directorate)
Maintenance
Initiation
ENHANCED JOINT WARFIGHTING CAPABILITY
JOINT DOCTRINE PUBLICATION
Approval
Development
STEP #3 - Approval
• JSDS delivers adjudicated matrix to JS J 7
• JS J 7 prepares publication for signature
• JSDS prepares JS staffing package
• JSDS staffs the publication via JSAP for signature
STEP #2 - Development
• LA selects primary review authority (PRA) to develop the first draft (FD)
• PRA develops FD for staffing with JDDC
• FD comment matrix adjudication
• JS J 7 produces the final coordination (FC) draft, staffs to JDDC and JS via Joint Staff Action Processing (JSAP) system
• Joint Staff doctrine sponsor (JSDS) adjudicates FC comment matrix
• FC joint working group

www.ingramcontent.com/pod-product-compliance
Lightning Source LLC
Chambersburg PA
CBHW081326310526
45789CB00018B/2440